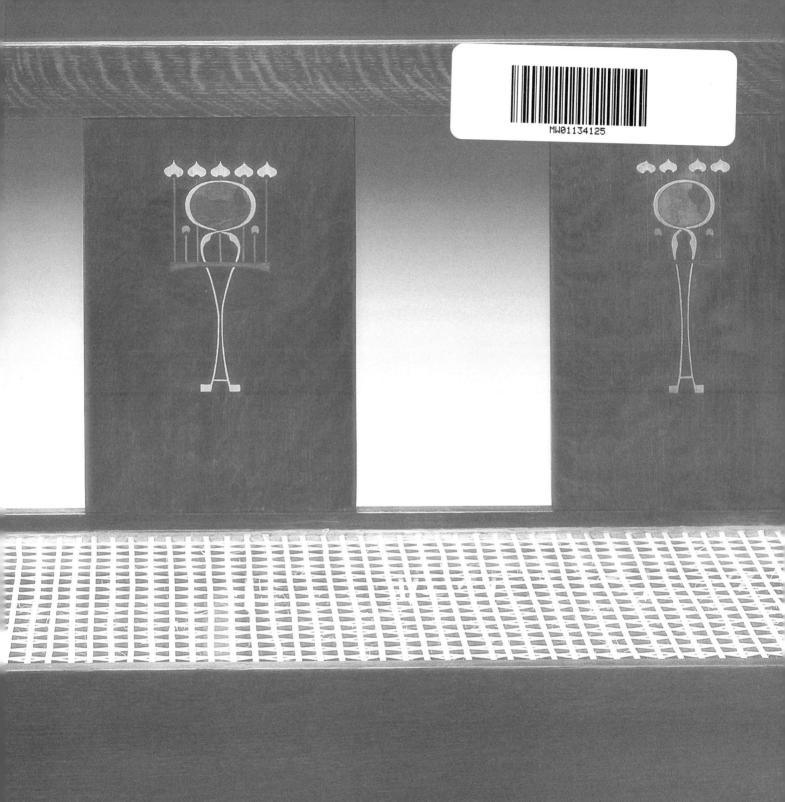

THE
STICKLEY
BROTHERS

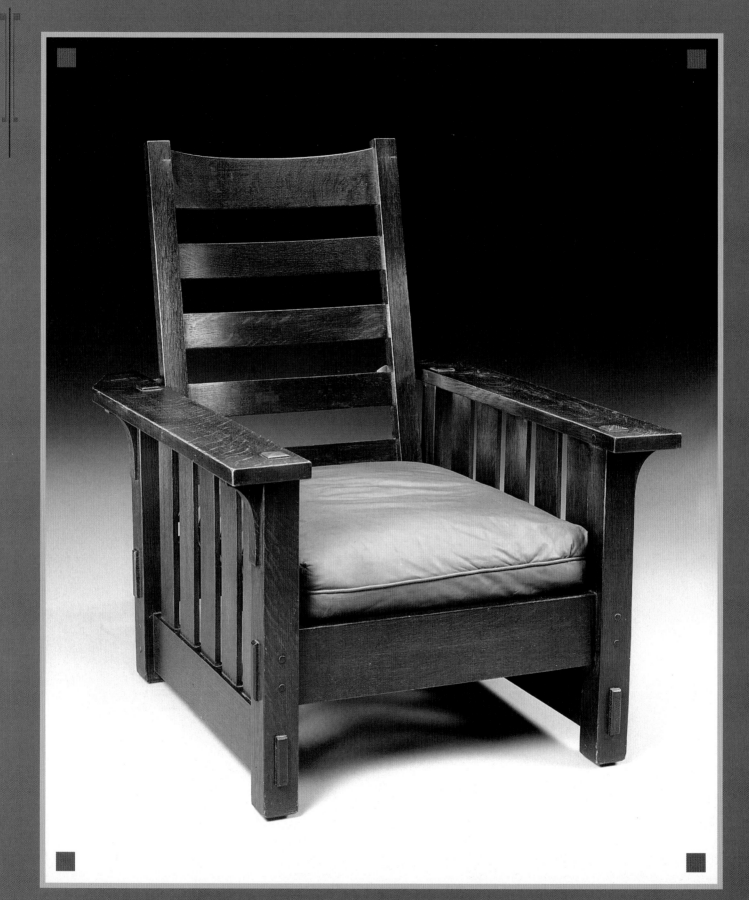

T H E
STICKLEY
BROTHERS

THE QUEST FOR
AN AMERICAN VOICE
▪ BY ▪
MICHAEL E. CLARK AND
JILL THOMAS-CLARK

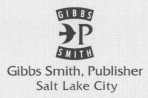

Gibbs Smith, Publisher
Salt Lake City

First Edition
06 05 04 03 02   5 4 3 2 1

Published by
Gibbs Smith, Publisher
P.O. Box 667
Layton, Utah 84041

Orders: (1-800) 748-5439
www.gibbs-smith.com

Cover design by O'Very-Covey
Interior design and production by Kurt Wahlner
Printed and bound in Hong Kong

Library of Congress Cataloging-in-Publication Data

Clark, Michael E.
  The Stickley brothers : the quest for an American voice / Michael E. Clark and Jill
Thomas-Clark. —1st ed.
     p. cm.
Includes bibliographical references and index.
  ISBN 1-58685-053-9
 1. Stickley family. 2. Arts and crafts movement—United States.
3. Furniture—United States—History—20th century. I. Thomas-Clark, Jill.
II. Title.
  NK2439.S79 C58 2002
  749.213'09'034—dc21
                        2002007578

**Tall case clock model 86, about 1910,
design attributed to Peter Hanson. This
clock is an interpretation of Gustav
Stickley's 1902 hall clock model 3.**

**Facing title page: Gustav
Stickley Morris chair model
2340, about 1901.**

C O N T E N T S

Detail of inlaid birds from the back panels of "Balmoral Settee," produced by Stickley Brothers.

FOR OUR PARENTS
JIM AND DOT CLARK;
JACK THOMAS

AND

IN MEMORY OF

JANET THOMAS

ACKNOWLEDGMENTS

It is impossible to put together a work such as this without the help of a large number of sources. Of course, we are deeply indebted to those who have gone before us, writing seminal works on the Stickley brothers. We are particularly indebted to Mary Ann Smith, Coy Ludwig, David Cathers, Donald Davidoff and Stephen Gray, Don Marek, Chris Carron, Cleota Reed, Pat Bartinque, Peter Copeland, and Marilyn Fish. These individuals, through their own scholarly works, museum shows and reissued catalogs, have laid the foundations for much of what is here. We have sought their counsel on the brothers over the years, and they have freely given information and advice.

Among other experts on the Stickley brothers and their work, many antiques dealers and collectors have given freely of their time and knowledge. It would be difficult if not impossible to name all who have shared bits and pieces of advice, but those who have been a constant source of advice and inspiration have been David Rudd, Bill Lower, Paul Horan, George and Karin Look, Jim Messineo, Linda Cunningham, and Norman Weinstein. We would also like to acknowledge the members of the Arts and Crafts Society of Central New York for their continued support and assistance. A particular note of thanks also goes to David Rago, who occupies a special place for us because of our work over the years with *Style 1900*. David's dedication, and that of his staff at *Style 1900*, to the Arts & Crafts movement is unquestioned, and his advice has always been inspirational and honest. Without David's support, this work would not exist.

We would also like to recognize the assistance of the following libraries and the dedicated librarians who have helped us to ferret out primary source material for this work. Carl Voncannon and his staff have graciously shared the resources of the Bernice Bienstock Furniture Library in High Point, North Carolina, and assisted us with our research for over eight years. The extensive collections of the Grand Rapids Public Library and especially the knowledge of Christine Byron have been invaluable. Both the Library and archival collections of the Winterthur Museum Library and the experience if its staff, including Neville Thompson, were of great help. The collections of the New York Public Library and the Onondaga Public Library were also exceptionally helpful. Without these resources, our work would have floundered.

We are especially grateful to Beth Ann McPherson of Craftsman Farms, Jennifer Doyle of Christies Images, Ross Van Pelt of Treadway Auctions, Amanda Jacobs and Suzanne Sliker of Craftsman Auctions for facilitating the loan of images of the works created by the Stickley brothers. We would again like to recognize Michael Danial, the corporate historian of the L. & J. G. Stickley Company, for his advice and comments. We are deeply indebted also to Alfred and Aminy Audi, the owners of L. & J. G. Stickley, for not only providing us with quality images for this work but also for their openness in giving us access over the years to their information and source material. Such assistance is clearly in the tradition of the cooperation that was shared among the Stickley brothers.

A special note of thanks also goes to Bruce Johnson, coordinator of the annual Arts & Crafts Conference at the Grove Park Inn in Asheville, North Carolina. Bruce has always provided us with invaluable advice and support on this and other projects. The gathering in Asheville each year has laid a strong foundation for our own knowledge of the movement.

Our employers also deserve a place here for their support and help in this project. The Corning Museum of Glass in Corning, New York, has provided support through their facilities and staff. Both have allowed us special access to primary source material and advice. Finally, our deep indebtedness to Elmira College, in Elmira, New York, for providing the special funding and a sabbatical leave to complete this project. The history of the decorative arts movement in America owes this institution a special footnote of gratitude.

The Voice and the Players

During the latter part of the twentieth century, the name Stickley achieved mythic proportions in the American decorative arts. Particularly since the landmark Princeton exhibit on the Arts & Crafts movement in America in 1972, it has become legendary and influential in modern American design. A virtual boom in modern reproductions and imitations of Arts & Crafts objects and furniture has permeated the American environment. Scholarship and research into the period has produced a plethora of knowledge about the artists and artisans of the early twentieth century. But until now, no one work has covered the impact of all five Stickley brothers on creating an American style in the decorative arts.

Born to Leopold and Barbara Schlager Stoeckel in the Wisconsin wilderness between 1858 and 1865, the five Stickley brothers (Gustav, Charles, Albert, Leopold, and John George) were destined to reshape our environment in new and innovative directions. As we shall see, even in their own lifetimes they achieved fame, their names becoming synonymous with the blossoming Arts & Crafts movement. These individuals, working both together and independently in the decorative arts, represent a microcosm of the national stylistic voice of America. At the turn of the twentieth century, the microcosmic voice of the Stickley brothers joined with others to change the environment of our homes. Like many artists at the beginning of the twentieth century, they were setting out to find an American style that mirrored her culture and soul. That journey is reflected in their innovative work and writings. It will be the goal of

Dining room in Mariposa, formerly the Frost-Tufts house (1911), Hollywood, California. The leather-back chairs by the window and chestnut dining table were created by Onondaga Shops, while the ladder-back chairs, the small trestle table by the window and the sideboard in the corner were produced by Gustav Stickley.

Gustav Stickley
(1858–1942).

this work to trace the quest of these brothers to find an American voice through their craft.

Of the five brothers, Gustav Stickley (1858–1942)[1] and Albert Stickley (1862–1928) represent the articulate, American industrial empire builders on a national and international scale respectively. Charles Stickley (1860–1927) and Leopold Stickley (1869–1957)[2] exemplified the practical furniture men. Charles was the brother who stayed behind in the shadows, while Leopold was the capable and functional survivor. The youngest of the brothers, John George (1871–1921), was the consummate American salesman who, at one time or another, marketed the ideas and goods of all the brothers. Each of the brothers performed his representative role as a player on the stage of the American Arts & Crafts movement.

Harmonies and Conflicts Among the Players

While enacting the various positions, the brothers all had similarities and differences in their approaches to the voice and style of their craft. Over the years, the evolutionary change in each brother's approach is reflected in his design and production. The resulting harmonies and conflicts represent the shaping of the American voice and the style of the movement as it was portrayed on a national scale.

Gustav Stickley is the best known of the five brothers. Unquestionably, he is the reason we currently hold an almost iconic reverence for the Stickley name in the history of the decorative arts. Gustav felt that he had found the source of American style in decorative design and had recreated it in his own work. On the third anniversary of the establishment of the *Craftsman,* the magazine he published to disseminate his ideas, Gustav wrote with a religious fervor about the basic American principle in style that prompted his "Craftsman" furniture. Taking pride in being "an American by birth," he wrote:

> Since the genius of the American is structural, as is proven by his government, his control of natural resources, his mastery of finance, let the building art—the lesser as well as the greater—provide him with surroundings in which he shall see his own powers reflected. In the appointments of his dwelling, let the structural idea be dominant, and the materials employed be, as far as is possible, native products, in order that the scheme may be unified and typical—above all, democratic.[3]

Although over the years his ideas continued to evolve, this structural principle of minimal or no adornment would remain the basis of his design. This principle of simplicity shaped his early career as a cabinetmaker. It is also interlinked with his brothers' principles and affected the development of their designs. However, the important question is did the creations of Gustav or any of his brothers reflect the birth of an American style?

The third brother, Albert, was also a dominant force in the furniture industry, shaping it on both a national and international scale. Albert, one of the major players in the Grand Rapids furniture industry, was the only brother who extensively marketed his goods overseas. Grand Rapids

1. Gustave Stickley dropped the final e from his name at the turn of the century. His familiar name was Gus. We have opted throughout this work to use Gustav except in quotes or when used as the title for his early company, The Gustave Stickley Company.

2. Leopold Stickley is familiarly known as Lee but his name also appears as Leo. Except in quotations, we have referred to him as Leopold.

3. Gustav Stickley, "Thoughts Occasioned By an Anniversary: A Plea for a Democratic Art," *Craftsman,* Oct. 1904, 48.

4. Frank Edward Ranson, *The City Built on Wood: A History of the Furniture Industry in Grand Rapids, Michigan, 1850-1950* (Ann Arbor, Michigan: Edward Brothers, Inc., 1955), 52.

became the American center of the web that fed a growing nation with household furnishings. In 1910, at the apex of the Arts & Crafts craze in America, it boasted fifty-four companies that employed 7,250 workers and had a net capital of $13,322,000.[4] It is clear why the Bureau of the Census noted in 1910 that Grand Rapids was "the recognized center of the furniture industry in the United States." (Cited in City, Ransom, p. 53) The "value of the product was $12,630,000 with an additional value of the manufacturer to the product of $7,693,000." In 1891, Albert Stickley thrust himself into this competitive market and remained there until shortly before his death in 1928.

Like his older brother Gustav, Albert drew upon English influences and sought to establish a twentieth-century style. He borrowed the English term "quaint" to define his style of furniture and goods. Unlike Gustav, Albert saw America as moving toward establishing a style. For Albert, however, that was a task yet to be completed. Using many of the same patriotic images evoked by Gustav, Albert pointed out in his own documents that the development of a true style was a slow, evolutionary process that required time and that we had only begun that process. Only three years before his death in 1928, he noted that style "changes . . . according to the trend of society, growth and development of national institutions, human liberties and social and economic progress . . . In the past one thousand years a tremendous change has come into the society of mankind. It was begun by the English, adopted by the French and completed, or nearly so, by the Americans."[5] In the closing passages of this document he declared:

5. Albert Stickley, *Adapting Quaint Furniture To American Needs* (Grand Rapids, Michigan: Stickley Brothers Company, 1925), 22.

> To say that American furniture is an established reality would be making a broad assertion. We have not had the time to develop a distinct American style. National traits, habits or arts are not formed overnight. They must have foundations, sometimes very old foundations. There is nothing antique in America, save a few Indian relics and the remains of prehistoric animals. We have not existed long enough as a nation to warrant the archaeologist in digging up our past or in rattling the skeletons of our ancient rulers.
>
> But we have developed in our furniture design and construction certain pleasing traits which are gradually and slowly forming themselves into a style. In other words, we are following the true history of furniture. We are doing for the American people what Boule did for the French, what the brothers Adam, Chippendale, Hepplewhite and Sheraton did for the English—taking the best from the past and making it conform to present needs. We are adapting furniture to our requirements and changing it to meet our finest understanding of what is beautiful and serviceable.[6]

6. Ibid., 24.

Albert's argument for American art and design was not a new one. He recognized the influences of European and other outside forces that were prevalent in the diversity of American design. However, Albert had a penchant for British design that may have biased his views. Although he survived the change from Arts & Crafts to other forms, his younger brother Leopold was a better adapter and survivor.

Despite Albert's pronouncements, many have given Gustav Stickley credit for developing the

Left:
Albert Stickley
(1862–1928).

Right:
Charles Stickley
(1860–1927).

first voice in American design. This has led Donald Davidoff to focus on the long-underestimated achievements of Leopold and John George. He notes, "Furniture produced by his [Gustav Stickley's] workshops represents classic American design and in some circles is considered to be the first original expression of American thought in furniture."[7] Citing the continuing seminal work of David Cathers, Davidoff qualifies his statements by pointing out that an analysis of Gustav Stickley's independent design work "reveals his debt to the English cottage revival style and the subsequent stylistic modifications he made over that span of years."[8] His thesis is that "it remained for the superior business acumen of his younger brothers, Leopold and John George, to place physical examples of [Gustav's] philosophy in middle-class American homes and to revitalize the entire 'mission aesthetic' for the second decade of the twentieth century."[9] The significance of the contribution of Leopold and John George was their ability to market the Arts & Crafts line that they created to the larger mass of people untouched by Gustav Stickley.

Davidoff, like David Cathers, credits some of the design innovations previously attributed to the Stickleys to various designers in their employ. It is well known that Harvey Ellis played a significant role in the changes in Gustav Stickley's work after 1903. Recently, Cathers has pointed to the design work of LaMont A. Warner and George H. Jones' marquetry for Gustav as being important innovations attributed to Gustav.[10] Around 1907, Leopold hired Peter Hansen, who had worked for Gustav Stickley. Davidoff has shown that Hansen was responsible for at least some of the innovative designs of Leopold's work during his mature period. Donald Marek has discussed several designers employed by Albert Stickley over the years, including David Robertson Smith and Arthur E. Teal.[11] Time and further research will no doubt uncover additional contributions by other designers in the innovations of the Stickley brothers.

7. Donald Davidoff, "Maturity of Design and Commercial Success," in *Substance of Style*, ed. Bert Denker (Winterthur, Delaware: Henry Francis du Pont Winterthur Museum, 1996), 161.

8. Ibid.

9. Ibid., 162.

10. David Cather's articles in *Style 1900*, "From the Studio of LaMont A. Warner," November 1996, 44-48, and "Gustave Stickley, George H. Jones & the Making of Inlaid Craftsman Furniture," February 2000, 54-60.

11. Don Marek and Richard Weiderman, "Introduction," in *The 1912 Quaint Furniture Catalog* (Parchment, Michigan: Parchment Press, 1993), vi-viii.

"Quaint Furniture" dining room designed by Arthur E. Teal for Stickley Brothers as seen in the *Grand Rapids Furniture Record.* Teal's monogram appears in the lower left corner.

■ ■

Gustav Stickley oak and leaded-glass china cabinet, model 964, 1902, design attributed to LaMont A. Warner.

What may be more significant is the interplay between the Stickley brothers during the transition in American design at the turn of the twentieth century. Each brother played a role in the developing saga. Even Charles, who lived out his life in his factory and retail store, enacted a specific part in the ensemble. As each brother left the confines of home, it was Charles who remained with his mother Barbara in Binghamton. It was there he formed his own company with friend and relative Schuyler Coe Brandt. Charles ran both a retail establishment and a factory where he designed a variety of styles from the traditional English lines to Art Nouveau. Although he did not enter the Arts & Crafts arena until later and modeled many of his designs after those of his brothers, some of his designs were distinctly different from the work of Albert, Gustav, Leopold, or John George. His "Modern-Craft" Arts & Crafts line, marketed in 1909, allowed John Towse to note: "The entire Stickley family is now engaged in the manufacture of mission and Arts & Crafts furniture. People in the trade have wondered why Charles Stickley didn't get into the game and make it unanimous. He had thought about it, all right, and last fall [1909] he finally got busy." [12] Although much of his work was imitative of his brothers' work, Charles also created some independent designs. He remained practical in his approach with a diversified production line until he went bankrupt in 1918 like his older brother. Nevertheless, for a few years, all the Stickleys were working separately but in unison on what may have been a new American concept in decorative design.

In subsequent chapters, we will examine the work of each of the brothers and their growth. They were a family, interlocked by blood and heritage. They came from similar environments but played different roles in the setting. There were differences and conflicts, but there were also similarities and harmonies in their search for a way to express themselves through their craft. The examination of this expression will answer the fundamental question of whether any or all of the Stickley brothers created an enduring American style.

12. John Towse, "On the Road," *Furniture World,* 16 December 1909, 11.

A TIMELINE OF THE STICKLEY BROTHERS

1850　　1860　　1870　　1880

Major
Exhibits

● **1876:** Centennial Exposition in Philadelphia, Pennsylvania.

● **1876:** Stickley family returns to Pennsylvania.

GUSTAV STICKLEY
Stickley Brothers Chair Company →

● **1858:** Gustav Stickley born in Osceola, Wisconsin.

● **1876:** Gustav employed at the Schlager family chair factory.

● **1883:** Gustav, Charles and Albert form the Stickley Brothers Chair Company in Susquehanna County, Pennsylvania.

● **1884–85:** Gustav, Charles and Albert move to Binghamton, New York; the three brothers operate a retail store and small chair factory in Binghamton.

CHARLES STICKLEY
Stickley Brothers Chair Company →

● **1860:** Charles Stickley born in Osceola, Wisconsin.

ALBERT STICKLEY
Stickley Brothers Chair Company →

● **1862:** Albert Stickley born in Osceola, Wisconsin.

LEOPOLD STICKLEY

● **1869:** Leopold Stickley born in Osceola, Wisconsin.

JOHN GEORGE STICKLEY

● **1871:** John George Stickley born in Osceola, Wisconsin.

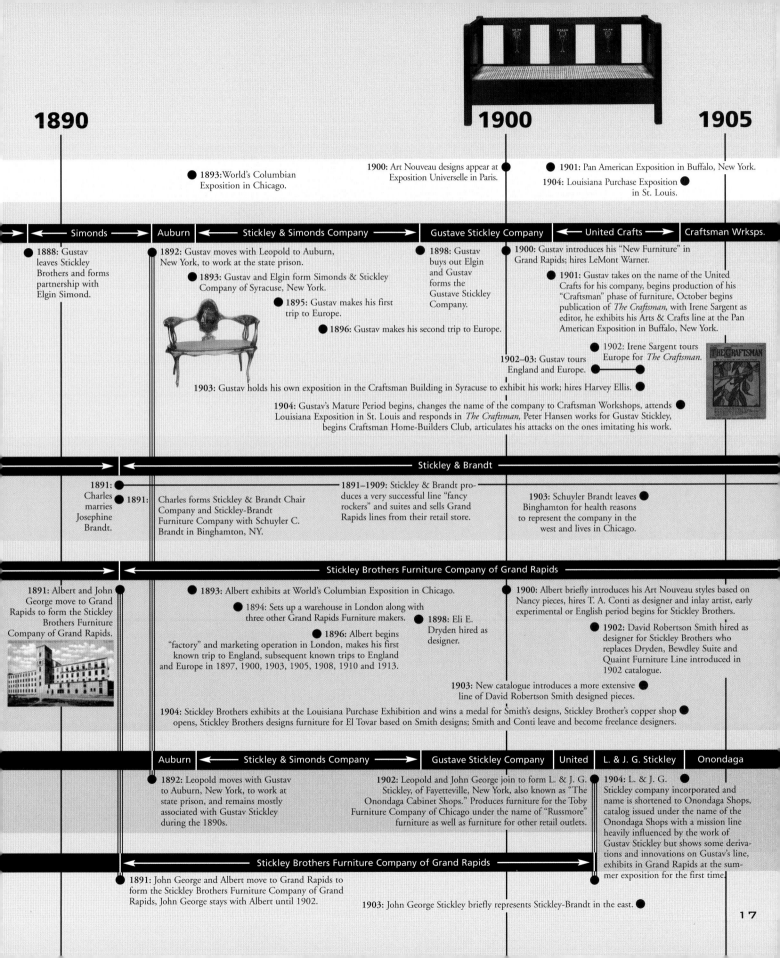

1890 **1900** **1905**

1893: World's Columbian Exposition in Chicago.

1900: Art Nouveau designs appear at Exposition Universelle in Paris.

1901: Pan American Exposition in Buffalo, New York.

1904: Louisiana Purchase Exposition in St. Louis.

← Simonds → | ← Auburn | ← Stickley & Simonds Company → | Gustave Stickley Company | ← United Crafts → | Craftsman Wrksps.

1888: Gustav leaves Stickley Brothers and forms partnership with Elgin Simond.

1892: Gustav moves with Leopold to Auburn, New York, to work at the state prison.

1893: Gustav and Elgin form Simonds & Stickley Company of Syracuse, New York.

1895: Gustav makes his first trip to Europe.

1896: Gustav makes his second trip to Europe.

1898: Gustav buys out Elgin and Gustav forms the Gustave Stickley Company.

1900: Gustav introduces his "New Furniture" in Grand Rapids; hires LeMont Warner.

1901: Gustav takes on the name of the United Crafts for his company, begins production of his "Craftsman" phase of furniture, October begins publication of *The Craftsman*, with Irene Sargent as editor, he exhibits his Arts & Crafts line at the Pan American Exposition in Buffalo, New York.

1902: Irene Sargent tours Europe for *The Craftsman*.

1902–03: Gustav tours England and Europe.

1903: Gustav holds his own exposition in the Craftsman Building in Syracuse to exhibit his work; hires Harvey Ellis.

1904: Gustav's Mature Period begins, changes the name of the company to Craftsman Workshops, attends Louisiana Exposition in St. Louis and responds in *The Craftsman*, Peter Hansen works for Gustav Stickley, begins Craftsman Home-Builders Club, articulates his attacks on the ones imitating his work.

← Stickley & Brandt →

1891: Charles marries Josephine Brandt.

1891: Charles forms Stickley & Brandt Chair Company and Stickley-Brandt Furniture Company with Schuyler C. Brandt in Binghamton, NY.

1891–1909: Stickley & Brandt produces a very successful line "fancy rockers" and suites and sells Grand Rapids lines from their retail store.

1903: Schuyler Brandt leaves Binghamton for health reasons to represent the company in the west and lives in Chicago.

← Stickley Brothers Furniture Company of Grand Rapids →

1891: Albert and John George move to Grand Rapids to form the Stickley Brothers Furniture Company of Grand Rapids.

1893: Albert exhibits at World's Columbian Exposition in Chicago.

1894: Sets up a warehouse in London along with three other Grand Rapids Furniture makers.

1896: Albert begins "factory" and marketing operation in London, makes his first known trip to England, subsequent known trips to England and Europe in 1897, 1900, 1903, 1905, 1908, 1910 and 1913.

1898: Eli E. Dryden hired as designer.

1900: Albert briefly introduces his Art Nouveau styles based on Nancy pieces, hires T. A. Conti as designer and inlay artist, early experimental or English period begins for Stickley Brothers.

1902: David Robertson Smith hired as designer for Stickley Brothers who replaces Dryden, Bewdley Suite and Quaint Furniture Line introduced in 1902 catalogue.

1903: New catalogue introduces a more extensive line of David Robertson Smith designed pieces.

1904: Stickley Brothers exhibits at the Louisiana Purchase Exhibition and wins a medal for Smith's designs, Stickley Brother's copper shop opens, Stickley Brothers designs furniture for El Tovar based on Smith designs; Smith and Conti leave and become freelance designers.

Auburn | ← Stickley & Simonds Company → | Gustave Stickley Company | United | L. & J. G. Stickley | Onondaga

1892: Leopold moves with Gustav to Auburn, New York, to work at state prison, and remains mostly associated with Gustav Stickley during the 1890s.

1902: Leopold and John George join to form L. & J. G. Stickley, of Fayetteville, New York, also known as "The Onondaga Cabinet Shops." Produces furniture for the Toby Furniture Company of Chicago under the name of "Russmore" furniture as well as furniture for other retail outlets.

1904: L. & J. G. Stickley company incorporated and name is shortened to Onondaga Shops, catalog issued under the name of the Onondaga Shops with a mission line heavily influenced by the work of Gustav Stickley but shows some derivations and innovations on Gustav's line, exhibits in Grand Rapids at the summer exposition for the first time.

← Stickley Brothers Furniture Company of Grand Rapids →

1891: John George and Albert move to Grand Rapids to form the Stickley Brothers Furniture Company of Grand Rapids, John George stays with Albert until 1902.

1903: John George Stickley briefly represents Stickley-Brandt in the east.

1 7

1905   **1910**

Major
Exhibits

Craftsman Wrksps. ←———————————— **Craftsman** ————————————→ **Assoc. Cabinet Makers**

● **1905:** Gustav patents his spindle chairs.

● **1906:** Gustav begins to work in his New York City offices, the "Craftsman" name becomes the registered name for the company.

● **1910:** Moves family to Craftsman Farms in New Jersey, begins his Final Production Period, loses court case to Kaufmann Brothers over design infringements.

● **1913:** Opens the Craftsman building in New York City.

● **1914:** Introduces his Chromewald furniture designs.

● **1915:** Gustav Stickley declares bankruptcy.

1916: Last issue of *The Craftsman* published. ●

● **1917:** Forms The Associated Cabinet Makers with Albert, Leopold and John George, it dies by 1918.

1918: ●
Retires to Syracuse to the Columbus Street home.

Stickley & Brandt ————————————————————————————→

● **1909:** Charles Stickley introduces his first mission line, "Modern Craft," so that all the brothers are now producing mission furniture, issues his first mission catalogue, introduces the Flanders line in an answer to the trend toward historical styles.

● **1913:** Schuyler Brandt dies in Chicago.

● **1917:** Ceases to produce mission furniture.

● **1918:** Stickley & Brandt goes into receivership and bankruptcy.

Stickley Brothers Furniture Company of Grand Rapids ————————————

● **1906:** Stickley Brothers begins marketing their furniture for the "entire house," and the mature period begins for Stickley Brothers.

● **1908:** Arthur E. Teal is hired as the company designer.

● **1909:** Stickley Brothers Tudor line is introduced as shift away from mission furniture begins with the introduction of range of historical styles.

● **1913:** Stickley Brothers introduces its Manor line of furniture but continues to produce a weakened mission line until the end of the decade.

● **1917:** Forms The Associated Cabinet Makers as a sideline with Gustav, Leopold and John George, it dies by 1918.

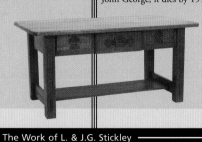

Onondaga Shops → ←— **Handcraft** —→ ←————— **The Work of L. & J.G. Stickley** —————

● **1907:** Handcraft name adopted for the L. & J. G. Stickley line, full line of furniture for den, library, and dining room appears, all work is done in a mission or Arts & Crafts design, Peter Hansen becomes the designer for the company.

● **1910:** L. & J. G. Stickley Furniture lines reach their full maturity, open larger showrooms in New York City.

● **1912:** L. & J. G. Stickley introduce their Prairie style settles and chairs, and cease using the Handcraft label in favor of The Work of L. & J. G. Stickley.

● **1917:** Forms The Associated Cabinet Makers as a sideline with Gustav, Albert and John George, it dies by 1918.

Onondaga Shops → ←— **Handcraft** —→ ←————— **The Work of L. & J.G. Stickley** ——→ **JOHN G**

● **1905:** L. & J. G. Stickley open their first New York City salesroom.

● **1906:** Last Onondaga Shops catalog issued.

● **1909:** New L. & J. G. catalogue/retail plates issued that show a bedroom line being made.

● **1917:** Associated Cabinet Makers.

● **1917:** L. & J. G. introduce their Shaker chairs and begin shift to their colonial reproductions.

A Timeline of the Stickley Brothers

1920   **1930**   **1940**   **1950**   **1960**

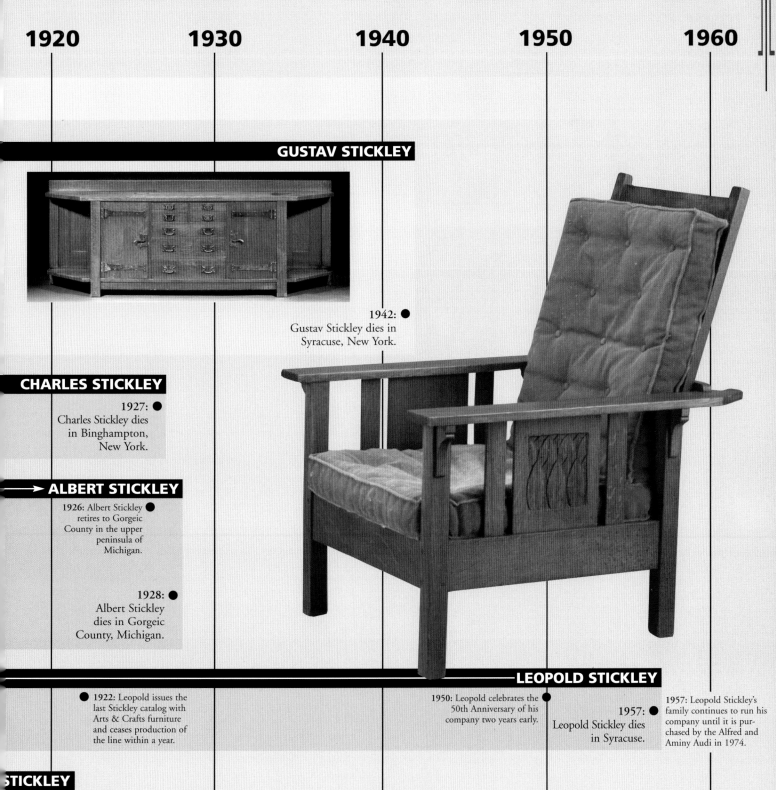

GUSTAV STICKLEY

1942:
Gustav Stickley dies in
Syracuse, New York.

CHARLES STICKLEY

1927:
Charles Stickley dies
in Binghampton,
New York.

ALBERT STICKLEY

1926: Albert Stickley
retires to Gorgeic
County in the upper
peninsula of
Michigan.

1928:
Albert Stickley
dies in Gorgeic
County, Michigan.

LEOPOLD STICKLEY

1922: Leopold issues the
last Stickley catalog with
Arts & Crafts furniture
and ceases production of
the line within a year.

1950: Leopold celebrates the
50th Anniversary of his
company two years early.

1957:
Leopold Stickley dies
in Syracuse.

1957: Leopold Stickley's
family continues to run his
company until it is pur-
chased by the Alfred and
Aminy Audi in 1974.

STICKLEY

1921:
John George Stickley dies in
New York.

19

The First Twenty-five Years

Craftsman dining room with recessed sideboard and tile back splash, the *Craftsman*, November 1905.

The 1876 Centennial Exposition in Philadelphia was the first major demonstration of America's culture and business acumen. The focus of this exposition was on "the ingenuity and invention of the Americans which was to make them the mass-production centre of the world a few decades later."[1] Here American furniture companies exhibited their wares. Three where the machine dominated furniture production. According to Joel Lefever, it was these three companies that "helped machine assisted production of fine furniture to gain acceptance."[2]

After the Philadelphia exposition, the nation, although still trapped in the confines of the Victorian age, began a long, serious search for an independent artistic and cultural identity. This process of exploration led America through a period of muddled styles ranging from English Chippendale and Sheraton to exotic Moroccan and Japanese extravagancies. However, America was not alone in its search through the decorative excesses. England and the rest of Europe would often be the source

1. John Allwood, *The Great Exhibitions* (London: Macmillian Publishing Co., 1977), 56.

2. Joel Lefever, "They Make Furniture with Machinery," *Grand Rapids Furniture: The Story of America's Furniture City* (Traverse City, MI: Village Press, 1998), 33.

for the esoteric designs seen at the World's Fairs and various expositions that were held with increasing frequency. For example, the *Grand Rapids Furniture Record* pointed out the change in ideological distance. Before the 1900 World's Fair in Paris an unknown author noted:

> "Paree" is much nearer to Grand Rapids than when the great French Capital held its last exposition. In fact, the Chicago fair so demolished the lines and divisions of the world of peoples as to reduce the surface of the earth to a thing of insignificant distances so far as they affect the things of every day life.[3]

3. "What of the Future," *Grand Rapids Furniture Record*, 1 June 1900, 24.

Between the 1878 exposition in Paris and the 1883 exposition in Chicago, to the 1900 World's Fair in Paris, the world seemed to shrink as ideas were passed from nation to nation. These numerous expositions and trade shows accelerated the beginning of a global trade village on a larger scale.

Left:
Victorian interior, about 1890. This room is cluttered with an eclectic mix of Moorish, Renaissance, and Rococo furnishings while the walls are covered with frames of various shapes and styles.

Right:
Interior designed by M. H. Baillie Scott, International Studio, August 1900.

For England and Europe, the Victorian age caused an increased value to be placed on the decorative arts and furniture in the home. By 1876, Victorian taste reached into the nooks and crannies of every American domicile. Kenneth Ames has identified what drove the late Victorians' desire for furniture.[4] He indicates that beginning in about 1850, an increasing value was placed on household goods because of two strands of Victorian culture: the rise of gentility and the ideology of domesticity. He notes: "The rise of gentility means the process of which more and more Americans lived in a style and with possessions formerly associated with the aristocracy, with the gentry. The ideology of domesticity refers to a belief system that confined women to homes while simultaneously assigning to domestic environments paramount importance in the shaping of character and behavior."[5] From the notion of gentility, people felt ostentation represented a higher place in society and that elaborate daily rituals developed in the home increased the need for a greater amount of furniture to accompany them. As the amount of furniture and other goods increased, people's

4. Kenneth L. Ames, "Good Timing and a Flair for Leadership," *Furniture City*, 1998, 7-19.

5. Ibid., 8.

taste began to develop what Ames calls the "aesthetic of denseness." Interiors became more elaborate. "Believing that more was better, wealthy Victorians or those who wanted to appear wealthy gave their rooms a density we find almost inconceivable today. For we sit on the other side of a great aesthetic divide that occurred around 1900. Up until that time, household interiors had become increasingly dense."[6] However, mixed with density of the environment was the concept of domesticity, where "the home was celebrated as a repository for important social values."[7] This last value would evolve during the next twenty-five years and lead to a revolt against the complexity of Victorian life. This drive

6. Ibid., 13.

7. Ibid.

Above:
Interior of the ground-floor sitting room at The Orchard, C. F. A. Voysey's home in Chorleywood, Hertfordshire, England.

Opposite:
"L'Art Nouveau" interior created by Edouard Colonna for the Exposition Universelle, Paris, 1900, published in *Deutsche Kunst und Dekoration,* September 1900.

is the basis for Gustav Stickley's pleas for simplicity in life and the environment. It offers a direct contrast between the multifarious Victorian interiors and those of the Arts & Crafts movement in America.

Following England's lead during the next twenty-five years, America would foster a set of fledgling Arts & Crafts ideals based on a synthesis of its Shaker foundations and European heritage. In doing so, it became part of a slow-paced international movement. In England, the ideals were linked to the founders of the English Arts & Crafts movement, particularly to John Ruskin and William Morris and their followers, such as M. H. Baillie Scott and C. F. A.

Voysey. The counterparts for this expression in France and Belgium would be found in the Art Nouveau movement, in Scotland in the work of Charles Rennie Mackintosh, in Austria in the Viennese Secessionist school, and in Germany in the *Jugensteil.* By the first decade of the twentieth century, all of the various international trends became influential in shaping the diversity of the American Arts & Crafts movement.

The Stickley brothers became aware of these trends either through their trips abroad or by their extensive study of periodicals such as the *International Studio* or *Deutsche Kunst und Dekoration.* In addition, a variety of trade journals and vernacular publications such as the *Ladies' Home Journal* and *House Beautiful* supplied and traded ideas at a dizzying pace. This information, coupled with a widespread conservative reform movement, helped to set the standards for American tastes, resulting in an American synthesis of these ideas in design.[8] The Stickley family and the brothers would be thrust into the maelstrom of change that was churning on the eastern seaboard of America.

8. Wendy Kaplan, *The Art That Is Life: The Arts & Crafts Movement in America, 1875-1920* (Boston: Museum of Fine Arts, 1987), 93-98.

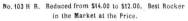

STICKLEY BROTHERS,

Manufacturers of Fine Antique and Fancy

CHAIRS,

ROCKERS

and SETTEES,

IN MAHOGANY, OAK AND CHERRY,

Would respectfully announce to those unacquainted with us that we have the reputation of making the very finest Goods at

MODERATE PRICES.

No. 103 H R. Reduced from $14.00 to $12.00. Best Rocker in the Market at the Price.

SEND FOR CATALOGUE.

BINGHAMTON, NEW YORK.

Advertisement for Stickley Brothers, Binghamton, NY, *American Cabinet Maker and Upholsterer,* March 2, 1889.

A NEW BEGINNING AND LEARNING A NEW CRAFT

During 1876, the year of the Philadelphia exposition, the Stickley family returned from Minnesota to their ancestral home in Pennsylvania.[9] Before moving to Wisconsin and on to Minnesota, the brothers' mother, Barbara Stickley, had lived in Pennsylvania with her family. There she was part of a distinguished lineage closely linked to the equally prestigious and wealthy Brandts. During a troubled marriage, Barbara returned to Lanesboro, Pennsylvania, to be near her family and her brother, Jacob Schlager. Although it seems that her husband, Leopold, returned for a short period, the separation was eventually complete. At that point, Barbara and her sons were on their own except for the help of relatives and friends.

Shortly after their arrival, Gustav was employed at the Schlager family chair factory in nearby Brandt, Pennsylvania. Within a few years, both Charles and Albert joined him. For the three brothers, it was a learning experience. Having been raised on farms in Wisconsin and Minnesota, all the brothers knew the value of hard work. And although the other brothers received at least the rudiments of a basic education, Gustav had to leave school to help support the family. He was trained as a stonemason, and he despised the work. Yet he constantly echoed the values taught by hard work. Gustav noted that the most valuable of all the arts was the art of living, which he had learned on the farm, working with nature. Gustav wrote:

> I learned when I was a very young lad that I could never fool Nature; that when I worked in the fields with her, in rain or sunshine or in wind, I was coping with the external elements, that I could not fake anything or talk back; that she was inexorable, that in order to achieve anything I must work with her; for I could never battle with her without being the sufferer.[10]

It was here in the mountains of northern Pennsylvania that the young Stickley brothers learned their initial skills in chair construction and the business of running a furniture company. While working in Brandt, the young men turned out the simplest of chairs, which, according to Gustav, were "the plain and cane-seated chairs so much used in those days." Although Gustav believed the work to be "stereotyped," it was from such tasks that he and his brothers learned the "appreciation" for wood and their craft.[11] The older Gustav became the foreman and "Charles became skilled in the weaving of rush fiber seats . . . while Albert showed skill in decorating old Boston rockers, which were among the products of the factory."[12] The work may have been stereotypical, but it was a reasonably up-to-date factory with all the proper machinery needed to crank out up to "8,000 dozen chairs per year."[13] This organization was characteristic of many of the furniture companies throughout much of the Northeast. It was small but productive and could be set up relatively inexpensively. Such small companies dotted much of the country, and the competition must have been keen for business.

By 1883, the three brothers set off on their own and formed the Stickley Brothers. With the help of their uncle, Jacob Schlager, and the family of Henry William Brandt, Jacob's longtime partner, they were able to raise the funds to set themselves up in business. In that same year,

9. Except where distinctly noted, in the following chapter I have closely followed Marilyn Fish's account of the family's early years in her two groundbreaking works, *Gustave Stickley: Heritage & Early Years* (North Caldwell, NJ: Little Pond Press, 1997) and *Gustave Stickley 1884-1900* (North Caldwell, NJ: Little Pond Press, 1999).

10. Gustav Stickley, "The Most Valuable of All Arts," *Craftsman*, September 1915, 528.

11. Gustave Stickley, *Chips from the Craftsman Workshops* (New York: Kalhoff Co., 1906) in Mary Ann Smith, *Gustave Stickley: The Craftsman* (Mineola, NY: Dover Publications, 1983), 2.

12. "The Tattler," *Furniture Journal* in David Cathers, *Furniture of the American Arts & Crafts Movement* (Philmont, NY: Turn of the Century Editions, 1996), 247.

13. Fish, *Heritage*, 27.

14. Stickley, *Chips*, 3.

15. See Fish, *Stickley: 1884-1900*, 9-22, for a detailed account of the changes and moves of the brothers during these years.

16. The dates for the end of the Binghamton plant and the start-up of the Syracuse plant remain muddled. A July 1892 advertisement in the *American Cabinet Maker and Upholsterer*, 27, notes that Stickley & Simonds Company furniture can only be seen at their factory in Auburn. An advertisement for the plant in Syracuse does not appear in the trade journal until May 6, 1893.

17. Apparently there is some question as to the exact date of the establishment of L. & J. G. Stickley's factory. Leo did work for himself or others during this period. For some notes on the argument see David Cathers, *Furniture of the Arts & Crafts Movement*, 75-76, and our later development of this topic.

the now-confident Gustav Stickley married Eda Ann Simmons. The following year, Charles and Albert moved to Binghamton to set up a branch of Stickley Brothers. By 1885, after they had sold the business in Brandt, Gustav joined his brothers in Binghamton.

It was at this point that they opened the retail store in Binghamton and, by 1886, established a chair factory in the attic of the store. According to Gustav Stickley, it was a primitive setup with only a bare minimal number of tools. Because of these limitations, he was forced to work in very simple Shaker and Colonial forms. He noted that it was "a golden opportunity to break away from the monotony of commercial forms." He felt that this period was the "foundation for original work along the same lines" that he "would do in the future."[14] The simplicity of the Shaker style of chair, unadorned and clearly American in design, became the foundation for his ideas. It is a form that he would continue to make until the turn of the century, when such ideas of simplicity would put him on the cutting edge of change.

The Stickley Brothers company, through diversification and ingenuity, became very successful in Binghamton. With the exception of Charles, each of the brothers would eventually leave Binghamton and become involved in his own enterprise.[15]

In 1887, Charles married Josephine Brandt, bringing together for the next generation the two families that had supported one another in the past. Shortly afterward, Albert married Jane Worden.

In December of 1888, Gustav left the Stickley Brothers firm and formed a partnership with Elgin Simonds. By January of 1891, Gustav and Elgin had started a plant in Binghamton. Then in 1892, Gustav, along with Leopold, moved to Auburn to become foremen of the prison furniture plant. In the meantime, the plant in Binghamton was closed and, with Elgin, Gustav established another factory in Eastwood, a suburb of Syracuse. Although the exact sequence of events is unclear, by at least 1893 the two had formed the Stickley & Simonds Company of Syracuse, New York.[16] Leopold worked with his brother in both Auburn and Syracuse almost continuously until he formed his own company in Fayetteville, New York in about 1902.[17] Gustav's relationship with Elgin continued until 1898, when Gustav struck out on his own to form the Gustave Stickley Company.

Although John George briefly joined Stickley Brothers in Binghamton, both he and Albert soon left for Grand Rapids where, in 1891, they established their own factory, retaining the family name, the Stickley Brothers Company. Around 1898, John George moved to New York City, where he married and continued to be vice president of the Stickley Brothers Company. During this period, he represented Charles as well. By 1902, John George joined forces with Leopold to form what would become the L. & J.G. Stickley Company. John George remained with Leopold until his death in 1921.

CHARLES STICKLEY: STAYING HOME

While four of the Stickley brothers made their mark on the furniture industry after moving away, it was Charles, the second oldest brother, who stayed behind. Charles had chosen to make his fortune in Binghamton within the shelter of his extended family, the Schlagers and the Brandts. Both locally influential families had deep roots in northeastern Pennsylvania and southern New York. They were politically powerful and involved in diverse business interests. The importance of the

STICKLEY & BRANDT CHAIR CO.,

BINGHAMTON, N. Y.

..MAKERS OF..

FINE AND MEDIUM

Chairs and Rockers,

Morris Chairs

PORCH AND SUMMER

··· Cottage Goods,

Den and Smoking Room Suits, Etc.

Advertisement with illustration of a fancy rocker for Stickley & Brandt Chair Company, Binghamton, NY, *American Cabinet Maker and Upholsterer,* May 6, 1899.

Stickleys' relationship with their kindred and its influence on all of the brothers' work should not be underestimated.[18] By staying behind, Charles was not only able to establish a thriving furniture factory and retail store, but he was also eventually able to follow in the footsteps of his brothers by creating a line of Arts & Crafts furniture—a line that was both derivative and innovative.

In 1891, faced with the changes in the family relationships, Charles Stickley and his cousin Schuyler C. Brandt founded the Stickley & Brandt Chair Company.[19] Shortly thereafter, the two men also formed the Stickley-Brandt Furniture Company.[20] This was the beginning of a strong friendship and close business relationship between the two men, one that echoed the family/business relationship of the last generation.

By 1891, Charles and Josephine had been married four years and had two children, Karl

18. Fish's work *Heritage* has demystified the impact of the strong family ties on the Stickley family.

19. Schuyler C. Brandt was the son of Henry William Brandt. The incorporation, with a capital stock of $30,000, was granted on December 30, 1891. Schuyler C. Brandt was president and Charles Stickley was manager.

20. The Stickley-Brandt Furniture Company was incorporated on December 22, 1896, with Schuyler Brandt as president and Charles Stickley as vice president. The company folded in 1928.

21. Barbara Stickley died on February 24, 1902, Williams *Binghamton City Directory 1902*, J. E. Williams of Binghamton, New York, 512. Throughout the years both she and Charles appear to have housed a number of other family members. The 1897 *City Directory* lists at least two others living with her, Christine B. Stickley, her daughter, and Tena Stickley, an unknown daughter or relative. Marie continued to live with her parents at the 124 Hawley Street address, as did Karl B. Stickley until his marriage to Julia in 1925/26.

22. *Grand Rapids Furniture World* and *Furniture Record* list exhibitors at the semiannual trade shows. Stickley & Brandt appear almost yearly throughout their existence from 1894 onward. For a note on the permanent exhibit and a listing of permanent exhibitors, see the advertisement in *Furniture World*, 22 February 1900, 1.

Brandt Stickley (b. ca. 1888) and Marie P. Stickley (b. ca. 1890). He would remain in Binghamton until his death in 1927. Tracing the family line through the city directories, it is clear that throughout the period Charles had the opportunity to remain in close contact with various family members as they moved in and out of both his mother's and his own home.[21]

Initially the Binghamton-based Stickley & Brandt Chair Company produced a line of simple chairs that were probably not much different from the ones produced by the original Stickley Brothers Company. Between 1890 and 1900, Charles, like his brothers, and Schuyler Brandt added historical revivals to their lines. The furniture factory manufactured fashionable chairs and settees, while the successful retail store they maintained in Binghamton sold a wide variety of goods from various Grand Rapids manufacturers including, of course, their own goods. The company exhibited their furniture at the New York and Grand Rapids furniture expositions on a regular basis. As early as 1894 they were exhibiting in New York. Surveys of both the *Grand Rapids Furniture Record* and the *Furniture World* from that period indicate that they seem to have been regular exhibitors at both shows at least once or twice each year. By 1900, they had set up a permanent New York exhibit of their line in the New York Furniture Exchange, which they kept well into the first decade of the new century.[22]

The early chairs shown in the Stickley and Brandt advertisements from this period were part of the fashion for historical revivals and fancy rockers. They show images of highly ornate chairs and English revivals of Chippendale or Sheraton. Throughout this period, there was a clamor for American and British "antiques." The word "colonial" was often used as a catchall term that referred to any reproduction from America's past. Such historical revivals, as well as the ornately carved "fancy rockers," were a mainstay of the period.

Advertisement for Veranda and Summer Cottage Furniture by the Stickley & Brandt Chair Company, the *Furniture World*, April 6, 1905.

According to the *Grand Rapids Furniture Record*, by 1895, the prosperous Stickley & Brandt Chair Company employed 160 men and was "rushed with orders." In spite of a fire in 1895 that destroyed a portion of the chair factory, the next five years saw remarkable growth in the company. In 1896, they had even hired a full-time designer. John Towse noted:

> Mr. Stickley tells me that George Miller, a most competent designer, by the way, is designing for the company a fine line of chairs, rockers and settees for the fall trade with a generous sprinkling of marqueterie pieces. The new goods will be shown in the Blogett building, Grand Rapids, in July.[23]

The use of inlay and highly carved and ornamental work was characteristic of the production of the company throughout much of this period. In 1897, the company moved into a new retail store that occupied four floors and a basement, making it one of the largest retail stores in the East. By 1900, they had also moved and expanded the chair factory as well. Charles Stickley noted: "We are moving out of one of the poorest factories into one of the very best, and we hope to do things."[24] The expansion of the factory was a major one. In the same article Stickley stated: "We employ 135 hands now, but will have room for between 300 and 400 after June 1." In the previous year, those 135 hands had turned out 45,000 chairs for the company. It was indeed a growing business.

The retail store continued to do well by selling its own goods as well as Grand Rapids furniture. Desks from the Standard Furniture Company of Herkimer, New York, were also sold, and were a staple in their store. This same company would win a Grand Prix medal at the World's Fair in Paris in 1900.[25] However, Stickley & Brandt's line does not seem to indicate any major influence from the English Arts & Crafts movement. After 1901, they do seem to have produced a number of pieces influenced by the 1900 World's Fair, and some of their "summer furniture" indicated an awareness of the Arts & Crafts movement. By 1901, their line was described as a "strictly high grade line of fancy chairs and rockers, including *L'Art Nouveau* innovations."[26] A quick survey of their 1902 catalog shows fancy rockers, Chippendale patterns, Victorian and Turkish couches, metal beds, office furniture, and a wide assortment of tables, dressers and other furniture. Their own designers created many of the chairs, but various Grand Rapids manufacturers made other items. However, at this point, no work was produced that was in any way similar in style or quality to the work created by the other brothers, either in Grand Rapids or in Syracuse. Charles would not emulate their new directions in furniture design until 1909.

ALBERT STICKLEY AND
JOHN GEORGE STICKLEY: EVERYTHING ENGLISH

In 1891, while Charles remained in Binghamton and Gustav was starting his business with Elgin Simonds, Albert and John George moved to Grand Rapids and formed the Stickley Brothers Company. The two brothers retained the name of the company initially organized in Binghamton and must have done well in the tradeoff and move. Once in Grand Rapids, they had enough capital

23. John Towse, "Everywhere," *Furniture World*, 30 April 1896, 27.

24. John Towse, "Everywhere," *Furniture World*, 26 April 1900, 28.

25. *Furniture World*, 13 June 1901, 10-11. Shows desks exhibited by Standard Furniture at the World's Fair in Paris, for which they won a Grand Prix award.

26. See "Stickley & Brandt Fire," *Furniture World*, 4 April 1895, 39; "Notes," *Furniture World*, 1 April 1897, 27; and "The Exchange Mirror," *Furniture World*, 24 January 1901, 27.

The Stickley
Brothers
plant in
Grand Rapids,
MI.

niture Co.,

U.S. 683.

STICKLEY BROTHERS COMPANY

Advertisement for Stickley Brothers Company, the *Furniture World*, December 30, 1897.

to build a large factory on Godfrey Avenue. According to Don Marek, the Stickley Brothers became significant players in the highly competitive Grand Rapids market. He notes:

> They began production in early 1892, making chairs and tables in typical styles of the time. [This would be historical revival chairs and tables similar to the work being done by the other brothers.] From initial capital of $100,000 and seventy-five employees, the Company grew rapidly. Gross sales the first year were $170,000.[27]

27. Don Marek and Richard Weiderman, "Introduction," *The 1912: Quaint Furniture Catalog*, Parchment Press, 1993, v.

28. Patent 550, 521. "Boiler-Cleaner," U.S. Patent Office, 26 November 1895, 1381.

29. *Grand Rapids City Directory*, (Grand Rapids: R. L. Polk & Co., 1896), 1034. The company Stickley and Myers was jointly owned by Albert Stickley, Leo Stickley and David Myers and was located at 36-38 Mill Street. In the 1897 *City Directory*, neither Leo Stickley nor David Myers is published in the company listing.

30. *Decorator and Furnisher*, September 1894, 233 in Fish, *Stickley: 1884-1900*, 21, 53.

31. John Towse, "Grand Rapids," *Furniture World*, 2 May 1895, 18.

Albert served as president of the newly formed company, while his brother, John George, the vice president, seems to have served principally as the company's sales representative. John George was called by many the "best fancy-rocker salesman" in the business. His role as salesman was one he seemed to relish. He would end up selling furniture for each of his brothers at some point in his career and at times represented more than one brother at once. It is clear he knew his product. For example, John Towse noted in 1904 that John George Stickley "can tell you more about the 'simple furniture,' how some of it is mortised and tenoned and wedged in five minutes than I could in a week." From 1894 until his move to New York in 1899, John George lived with Albert. In 1896, Leopold Stickley appeared in Grand Rapids, boarded with Albert, and, for at least a year, helped run a boiler purification plant owned by Leopold and David Myers. It seems that Myers, Albert, and Leopold all shared the patent for a device used to clean boilers.[28] Thus, a close communication between Albert and Leopold had been established in their business dealings.[29] It would be reasonable to conclude that such a pattern of interaction would continue over the years.

Within a year of commencing production, Albert began to take bold steps on an international scale that would eventually place him in the forefront of the American furniture industry. In 1893, along with several Grand Rapids manufacturers, he exhibited some of his production chairs at the World's Columbian Exposition in Chicago. By September of 1894, inspired by the response to the goods, he had joined forces with the Widdicomb Furniture Company, Stow and Davis Table Company, and the Grand Rapids Desk Company to set up a warehouse in Manchester, England.[30] By May of 1895, he had also made arrangements with Messrs. Navarro and Clark of the Argentine Republic "to handle Stickley Bros' chairs in the southern republic . . . and will probably perfect similar arrangements with other manufacturers here."[31] With Albert's increased international interest, what role did Albert play in the establishment of the warehouse, and what effect did it have upon any of his brothers?

Importantly, 1895 and 1896 were watershed years for both Albert and his brother Gustav. In the spring of 1895, Gustav returned from his first known visit to England. Approximately a year later, Gustav returned from his second trip to Europe.[32] In April of 1896, the following note appears in the *Furniture World*: "Gustave Stickley, of the Stickley & Simonds Co., Syracuse, N.Y. arrived in this port from Europe on the Majestic, Wednesday, April 1. Mr. Stickley brought home many fresh ideas which will be placed before the trade next season in the new line of chairs."[33] Next, according to John Towse in the August 27 issue of the *Furniture World*, we find that Stickley Brothers had opened a warehouse in London in the same year.

> Messrs. Stickley Bros Co., have opened a London warehouse, under the management of Mr. F. S. Tucker, at 71 Paul street, Finsbury (between Leonard square and Great Eastern street). In a circular to the trade they state that their object is to come in direct contact with the wholesale trade buyers of Great Britain, and by adopting English styles and manufactures most in favor, to secure the patronage of the trade, while at the same time presenting at first hand the most salable American specialties already introduced. In addition, therefore, to a line of roll-top desks, which will be found to be the most desirable in price, construction, and finish produced, they offer a few patterns of bedroom suites of superior workmanship and elegant finish, in various native woods, made after approved English designs. Also a large variety of house and office chairs, bookcases, music cabinets, dining-room and drawing-room tables, wardrobes, chiffoniers, and house desks.[34]

About a week later, Towse noted again Stickley's apparent ownership of a new warehouse and John Mowat's satirical response: "John Mowat of the Grand Rapids Chair Co., and Albert Stickley, of Stickley Bros. & Co., left Monday, Aug. 31, for New York. They sailed Sept 2 on the St. Louis for a six weeks' trip to England. Mr. Stickley goes on business in connection with his foreign establishment, and Mr. Mowat goes to keep him company. 'Just to see the elephant,' he says."[35] Below this entry appears a note that "John Widdicomb, of the Widdicomb Furniture Co., also sails for England Sept. 9, on a purely business trip."[36] Apparently, the warehouse was Albert's operation, although he was selling goods from other Grand Rapids furniture companies.

This convenient arrangement appears to have continued throughout the duration of the London establishment, even as it evolved into a factory where the goods were assembled. Subsequently, almost all references in the trade journals referred to it as being Albert Stickley's operation. For example, the men take a "short trip to the continent" with Mr. Widdicomb, where they visited various furniture factories in Germany, France, and the Netherlands. When the men return, Towse again pointed out that Mowat went with "Albert Stickley to look after the store of Mr. Stickley in London."[37] Again in 1897 Towse noted that "Albert Stickley has gone to London for a couple of months to look after his London store, which is doing lots of business. The foreign market was at last an accomplished fact and was the best kind of success."[38]

Maybe even just as important as Albert's success is a brief note a few pages earlier in the October 1896 issue of the *Furniture World*. Here the reporter notes: "Messers. Stickley and Simonds, of

32. Ellis Island Passenger Records, 192.168.1.86, 12 December 2001. Available from http://www.elisisland records.com.

33. John Towse, "Notes," *Furniture World*, 9 April 1896, 17.

34. John Towse, "Grand Rapids: Notes," *Furniture World*, 27 August 1896, 29.

35. John Towse, "Grand Rapids: Notes," *Furniture World*, 8 September 1896, 28-29.

36. Ibid.

37. John Towse, "Grand Rapids: Notes," *Furniture World*, 22 October 1896, 21.

38. John Towse, "Notes," *Furniture World*, 19 August 1897, 20.

Syracuse, N.Y. were in town last week, the latter looking over the market for orders, the former on pleasure bent." Apparently not only had Albert returned from England but also his brother Gustav was in town after having visited England in March and April of the same year. Gustav and Albert had made trips to England and Europe during the same year within months of each other. Gustav had made a trip in the previous year. It would be reasonable to conclude that Gustav and Albert discussed their ideas and what they saw on their travels after they returned in 1896. Perhaps Gustav was doing business for or with Albert on his trips. During Albert's trip, William Morris died (October 3, 1896) and a very brief obituary appeared in the *Furniture World*.[39] Ruskin and Morris's ideals would shape both Albert and Gustav's future design concepts. Perhaps they discussed the passing of Morris and his ideas. In the years to come, both men's ideas would evolve and be influenced by the Arts & Crafts design coming from England and Europe. The effect it had on them would put Gustav and Albert in the forefront of the movement in America.

During the years between 1891 and 1899, the products from Stickley Brothers of Grand Rapids do not seem to differ in any significant way from the fashionable furniture being done by the rest of the Stickley clan. The advertisements that appeared in the various trade journals did not denote any progression toward the Arts & Crafts movement. They publicized both a medium- and a high-priced line of artistic chairs and fancy tables. Their American design was not as important as their constant exposure to other designs in England and Europe.

What was more important for Albert during these years was Grand Rapids and his position in the industry. The advertisements from this period promote the Grand Rapids location of the factory and their permanent show/salesroom within the factory itself. Having a permanent showroom in the leading furniture city of America gave Albert's company a distinct advantage over other companies, including his brothers'. It was an enviable position that made him a major player in the industry.

During this period, Grand Rapids occupied a special position in the furniture industry. Albert's initial move to Grand Rapids was well thought out. As the population center of the United States moved farther west, and larger waves of skilled immigrants swept over the country, the Midwest flourished. Although large cities such as New York, Boston, and Philadelphia and smaller cities such as Syracuse all had numerous furniture factories, they were not predominant in the business community. However, the high concentration of furniture trade and furniture-related industries dominated the business activity of Grand Rapids. Kenneth Ames has pointed out that this concentration, along with the late development of the industries, aided in establishing a clear leadership position for Grand Rapids. The late establishment allowed Grand Rapids to avoid the pitfalls of having traditional, old-fashioned methods of production and the subsequent growing pains often felt when transitioning from the old traditions to the new ones. Ames also explains that because of the importance of the furniture industry to its economy, Grand Rapids developed a comprehensive library for the study of styles and the trade, an outstanding trade publication called the *Grand Rapids Furniture Record*, and a comprehensive furniture market. All of these combined brought a large number of retailers to Grand Rapids once or twice a year.[40] Albert Stickley had made an intelligent choice.

As a result, Albert's business prospered during this time, and his interest in England continued.

39. "William Morris, the celebrated English poet, died Oct. 3," *Furniture World*, 8 October 1896, 5.

40 Ames, "Good Timing," in *Furniture*, 16-19.

He remained in contact with his brothers and friends in Binghamton. John George and Leopold maintained close family ties to Binghamton and with their brother in Syracuse. For example, in June 1896, it was announced that "Albert Stickley is having plans made in Binghamton, N.Y. for a residence for himself on North Prospect Street."[41] Although the residence was to be built in Grand Rapids, he returned to Binghamton for his architect. Don Marek described the residence as "a pillared mansion in the Georgian style at 60 Prospect Street in Grand Rapids' Heritage Hill district, a favored location for wealthy businessmen."[42] Marek continues: "His choice of architectural style gives a clue to one of the defining traits of Albert Stickley: his love of things English."

41. John Towse, "Notes," *Furniture World*, 25 June 1896, 52.

42. Marek, "Introduction," *Catalog 1912*, v.

Albert Stickley's home at 60 N. Prospect Avenue, Grand Rapids, MI.

However, it is not until 1899 that we begin to get a hint of the effect Albert's penchant for English style had on his future designs and production methods. In June, after his return from one of his numerous visits to the London branch of the company's business, Albert's comments on trade with England were reported in the *American Cabinet Maker and Upholsterer*. He said bluntly that the popular style of furniture in England "is severely plain without any of the cheap 'ginger bread' work with which so much of the furniture on this side is adorned. The graceful lines and solid, substantial appearance of the English-made stuff shows unmistakably that we on this side have much yet to learn." He continued that the production system was different and that there were "few large factories . . . when compared with mammoth plants of some of the local companies. Most of the furniture is hand made . . . [and the] grade of the work turned out by them is much better than that done here by machinery." He concluded the interview by noting that they expected to make an exhibit at the Paris exposition in the following year "but will make it from our English office and with the English exhibit, because there will be no exhibit from this city."[43]

In January, Albert was back in London again on an extended trip through England, Germany,

43. "Albert Stickley on the English Furniture Trade," *American Cabinet Maker and Upholsterer*, 17 June 1899, 7-8. This interview originated in the *Grand Rapids' Herald* and was reprinted in abbreviated form in the *Furniture World*.

and France and "full of hope for the future of their European trade." When he returned, he described how the English style had changed his design work. Significantly, he pointed out the methodology and changes:

> Under present arrangements, we do from one-half to two-thirds of the work on our chairs after they reach London. All of the setting up, finishing and upholstering is done over there, and the product when completed has more the style of English manufacturers than it has of American. Just now the taste in England is tending toward a severely plain type. Carving over there detracts from the saleability [sic] and price of goods. We have shipped carved goods over and found we could have sold the same goods for more money if we had left the carving off. [44]

44. John Towse, "Mr. Albert Stickley Interviewed," *Furniture World*, 15 March 1900, 25.

He left the carving off, and the chairs sold well in England. Thus, what emerges from these interviews is an indication of the change to simplicity that was about to explode in American design. The Arts & Crafts design forms that were based on the philosophies of William Morris and John Ruskin existed before 1900. By 1897, Joseph P. McHugh had introduced his "Mission" furniture at his Popular Shop in New York. Other manufacturers, including the Michigan Chair Company, claimed that they created the first "Mission" chair and a lively debate developed. [45] The next few years would see popularization of the diverse forces that make up the Arts & Crafts movement. Albert would play a major role in disseminating the new designs as interpreted with an American voice. However, the brother that would speak first would be the dreamer, Gustav Stickley.

45. The argument about who introduced the first "Mission" furniture is a long and needless one. Most of the credit seems to go to Joseph P. McHugh, but there are other arguments for a host of others, including the Michigan Chair Company of Grand Rapids. See Anna Tobin D'Ambrosio, *The Distinction of Being Different* (Utica, NY: Munson-Williams-Proctor Institute, 1993), 18, 26, 35.

Interior of the chair factory at the State Prison, Auburn, NY.

GUSTAVE STICKLEY AND ELGIN SIMONDS: FASHION AND EXPERIMENTATION

The partnership of Gustav Stickley and Elgin Simonds seems to have been productive but was probably laced with tension. Like Albert, in 1891, Gustav and Leopold left Binghamton to become foremen for the furniture shop at the state prison in Auburn.[46] A year later, Gustav's wife and three daughters joined him. In the meantime, Gustav maintained his partnership with Simonds and, by 1893, had sold the factory in Binghamton and established one in Eastwood. His Eastwood plant would become the base of his furniture empire. Syracuse, a diverse and growing city, was very different from Grand Rapids. Marilyn Fish adequately describes the city when she notes:

> As for the future, Syracuse looked expectantly toward its commercial, intellectual, and industrial communities. Its downtown boasted many new, architecturally distinguished hotels, office buildings, and banks. Syracuse University founded in 1873 was positioned on a commanding hilltop, where its buildings symbolically bestowed wisdom upon the surrounding residential area. By 1892, its colleges of liberal arts, fine arts, architecture, and medicine, its library, museum, observatory, and gymnasium attracted artists, linguists, writers, scientists, and athletes from throughout the region. Meanwhile, by 1886 a manufacturing zone had formed around the city's perimeter . . . It seems from the start Gus was attracted to both the intellectual and industrial resources of Syracuse. His home was located one block from the University campus, while his factory was in the industrial belt that expanded into neighboring Eastwood.[47]

The growing city was larger and more diverse than Binghamton but, unlike Grand Rapids, it was not a city that was built on the furniture industry with well-attended biannual furniture markets.

46. As noted before, except where distinctly noted, I have closely followed Marilyn Fish's account of Gustav's years with Simonds and the establishment of The Gustave Stickley Company.

47. Fish, *Stickley: 1884-1900*, 20-21.

Three examples of Gustav Stickley's experimentation into "extreme" styles with Morris velvets. Manufactured by Stickley & Simonds, the *Decorator and Furnisher*. October 1895.

Albert was surrounded by a regional and international furniture industry, but Gustav was not.

Like his brother Albert's products, the early products Gustav turned out with Stickley and Simonds belonged to the mainstream of furniture design with the exception of some initial esoteric experimentation with historic styles. As early as 1893, trade journal advertisements indicated they were selling just about any type of chair imaginable in the popular, traditional historical styles. Towse noted:

> I went through the factory from start to finish. Full time, full complement of men, and everybody busy, from president to office boy. This company are [sic] making high grade stuff—Colonial, French Renaissance, Sheraton, Chippendale—purest of the pure, in oak,

Top row: Stickley & Simonds advertisement for their line of "High Grade" mahogany and oak historical revival chairs, the *Furniture World,* March 19, 1896.

mahogany and inlaid. One hundred and twenty new chairs were designed for the fall trade, and now they are making a supplementary line of a dozen patterns, extreme styles, but very aristocratic looking, upholstered in Morris velvets, colorings that match the dark, rich mahogany beautifully. One of these new pieces is illustrated in the company's advertisement in this issue. Elgin Simonds is going over his territory and picking up orders every day."[48]

48. John Towse,
Furniture World,
3 October 1895, 28.

As an aside, Towse concluded that Gustav Stickley had to give up riding his bike to work since he broke his arm. As a result of the break, Gustav had become "ambidextrous." In spite of his newly learned talent, it is clear from Towse's remarks that it was Gustav who was in charge of the factory

Lower row: Stickley & Simonds advertisement for their line of "High Grade" Colonial and Shaker revival chairs and rockers with enamel finishes, the *Furniture World*, March 19, 1896.

49. John Towse,
Furniture World,
9 April 1896, 17.

50. John Towse,
Furniture World,
28 April 1896, 82.

51. Fish, *Stickley and
Simonds*, 35.

52. John Towse,
Furniture World,
12 November 1896,
16. Walter Plumb
may have been hired
by Simonds because
when Gustav Stickley
and Simonds broke
off their relationship,
Plumb went with
Simonds to be the
designer for his new
firm.

53. Stickley & Simonds
advertisement in
Furniture World,
24 December 1896,

and that Elgin, like John George to Albert Stickley, was the salesman. Their products were traditional but bordered on the "extreme," using "Morris velvets." Such experimentation with form seems to have been inherent in the company and would eventually take on added importance. A few months later, we find illustrations of a "Lenox chair upholstered in Delft 'Morris' Velvet." Significantly, the use of "Morris Velvet" or William Morris fabric is Gustav's first-known use or connection to the English Arts & Crafts movement. The enameled and decorated finish on this chair, with its thinly spiked, Voysey-like rabbit ears and front posts, are imitations of the Shaker style with modifications.

After Gustav's second 1896 trip to Europe, Towse noted that Gustav had promised "fresh ideas which will be placed before the trade next season in the new line of chairs."[49] According to Towse, the result was a number of "new designs in antique chairs. Some of them are reproductions of rare patterns, some are brought out with modified lines and a number are of purest empire."[50] Marilyn Fish points out that another of the new designs was a "three-piece reception suite *a la vernis Martin*, that is, decorated in a style developed by the Martin brothers in France during the period of Louis XV. The Martins were famous for hand-painting pastoral scenes, in the style of Watteau and Boucher, on the solid-colored bodies of royal carriages, then applying a coat of specially formulated varnish for a crackled, or 'antiqued' finish."[51] Subsequent notes from Towse confirm that Stickley and Simonds did add new designs, and most appeared to be copies of the work seen in Europe. Gustav was now experimenting with historical styles, modifying their design or finish, just as he had done with the Shaker chairs, but now showing European influences and a new Arts & Crafts influence as well.

Interestingly, before the introduction of the new line, a new designer was hired. Towse noted in the *Furniture World*, "Walter Plumb designer who has been in the employ of M. F. & F. E. Schrenkeisen some months, has accepted an engagement with the Stickley & Simonds Co. Syracuse, N.Y."[52] Only a few months before, Gustav and Elgin had been in town with Elgin "looking over market orders" while Gustav was "on pleasure bent." As we presumed, the pleasure more than likely included a meeting with Albert after his return from Europe. What may be emerging from this picture is a Gustav Stickley who is prone to experimentation with his designs. What is mystifying is why a new designer would be hired just after Gustav returned from Europe with "fresh ideas" that evidently were being tested. In December of 1896, advertisements began to appear announcing that their "spring line [was] on exhibition only at factory."[53]

In January of 1897, various trade journals reported the production of two new lines—the Japanese and Egyptian bamboo suites. The Japanese suite evidently proved to be more popular with the public and was renamed the Villa suite. It was first pictured in the March 1897 issue of the *Upholsterer*. John Towse described this new line:

> At considerable expense Stickley & Simonds last January fitted up a department in the factory for the manufacture of bamboo work. Soon as samples were shown orders enough were booked to keep the department running to its capacity six months. A surprising variety of pieces is manufactured and the designs have the merit of being extremely tasty.

STICKLEY & SIMONDS CO.,

SYRACUSE, N. Y.

HIGH-GRADE NOVELTIES.   CHAIRS AND ODD PIECES FOR THE PARLOR,
HALL, LIBRARY, AND DINING-ROOM.   DINING CHAIRS,
ANTIQUE AND MODERN.

ILLUSTRATIONS FURNISHED.

85

The Villa Suite shown as "A Room in Forest-Green Furniture," the *Upholsterer.* March 1897.

WRITE US
For Cuts and Prices on the Best
MORRIS CHAIRS
MADE FOR THE PRICE.

ROD CAN'T KNOCK OUT.
You should see them before buying.
GUSTAVE STICKLEY CO.,
SYRACUSE, N. Y.

Morris chair from the cheaper line of goods introduced by Gustav Stickley, the *Furniture World*, February 16, 1899.

There are couches, tables, veranda benches, tabourettes, screens, bookcases, music cabinets, reception suites, etc., in 100 different styles. Numerous pieces are covered in Japanese figured matting, while others are upholstered in Oriental fabrics. Forest green seems to be a popular finish. These goods brighten up a retail stock wonderfully and make a pretty display. That they sell readily is proven by the business Stickley & Simonds are securing on the line.[54]

54. John Towse, "On the Road," *Furniture World*, 6 May 1897, 6.

The success of the Villa suite was followed by others in spite of advertisements that reminded the buyer that he must come to Syracuse to see all the new lines.

Although such advertisements may appear arrogant, the year of 1897 appears to have been a good one. During the year, a variety of new advertisements frequently appeared in the *Furniture World*, heralding the introduction of other new chairs into the line. The new work must have impressed people because in December of 1897 the company received a particularly important commission from the Waldorf Astoria Hotel in New York. According to John Towse, the commission called for them to outfit the foyer "where it [the furniture] will be constantly seen and commented upon. The sofas are massive mahogany pieces, ornamented and gilded with all the

Empire characteristics. Some of the pieces are copies, while others are original. It is furniture that will bear studying and the members of the company are justly proud."[55] In addition to furnishing the foyer, Towse indicates that they furnished café and suit chairs for the rooms, which kept the company busy working seven days a week.

The following year would be one of change in the Stickley & Simonds Company. In February of 1898, Elgin Simonds was in New York and "looking for business."[56] In the spring, Gustav evidently bought out his partner and by June it was announced that Elgin Simonds had bought out the Hayden & Couch Chair Mfg. Co. of Rochester, and that he was now president of the Brown & Simonds Company. The new company would be represented by both Sam and Elgin Simonds at the July Exhibition at the Pythian Temple in Grand Rapids.

Interestingly, advertisements for Stickley and Simonds continued to appear in the *Furniture World* until August 8, 1898, but with the date of April 7, 1898 listed at the bottom. On August 8, a new advertisement appeared listing the Gustave Stickley Company as "Successors to Stickley & Simonds Co."[57] These advertisements appeared on the inside cover of the *Furniture World,* the usual location for Gustav's advertisements. The inside cover was a more expensive location, and it is clear that he spent and relied heavily on well-placed advertising. He continued to advertise in the *Furniture World,* linking himself with the former Stickley & Simonds Company until January, when Gustav announced he would exhibit in the Pythian Temple in Grand Rapids. This was the first time that Gustav Stickley had exhibited since encouraging people to come to Syracuse to buy his goods. The new advertisement pictured a Morris chair and emphasized his line of such chairs that were "made for the price."[58] The Stickley and Simonds reference continued as late as May 1899 in the *American Cabinet Maker and Upholsterer.*

The reasons behind the split between Stickley and Simonds are only conjectural. Marilyn Fish attributes it to Gustav's seeking independence and a company of his own."[59] No doubt there was tension between Stickley and the more conservative Elgin Simonds, a hardworking salesman and respected member of the furniture industry. After leaving the company, Elgin continued his successful career selling traditional furnishings in a conservative fashion. On the other hand, Gustav Stickley, who had been in charge of the factory, had been praised for his "artistic" designs by the trade and had shown a tendency to take some moderate risks in design with his Japanese line. At this point, he briefly took a new tack by adding a cheaper line to his more traditional, more expensive line. In November of 1898, Towse praised the "marked individuality" of Gustav's designs but noted that "he had elected to serve the trade with cheap and medium priced chairs" but that he would continue to manufacture the more expensive grade as well.[60]

However, by May, Gustav had given up the idea of "cheap goods" and was designing an exclusive, more expensive line. Once again Towse noted: "It is conceded that Gustave Stickley possesses exquisite taste in the designing of graceful pieces, and his fancy seems to have been given a free rein in the conception of these handsome novelties."[61] In July, Gustav introduced his No. 2316 Morris Chair, which Towse extensively praised. He noted that the "peculiar feature which brands it as such is that the lines of the back are so drawn that it fits the sitter and assures solid comfort."[62] The chair, pictured

55. John Towse, "On the Road," *Furniture World*, 11 November 1897. Also see Fish, *Gustave*, 37, for her comment based on *The Upholsterer.*

56. John Towse, "Visitor's Register," *Furniture World*, 24 February 1898, 7.

57. The first "April 7" ad appeared on April 14 in the *Furniture World*, on the third page of the inside cover. The August 4 ad also appeared on the third page of the inside cover.

58. Advertisement in *Furniture World*, 16 February 1899, 11.

59. Fish, *Stickley: 1884-1900*, 38.

60. John Towse, "On the Road," *Furniture World*, 17 November 1898, 5.

61. John Towse, "On the Road," *Furniture World*, 11 May 1899, 6.

62. John Towse, *Furniture World*, 27 July 1899, 30.

for the first time in the July 1899 issue, is a more massive Morris chair than seen before, with open arms and shoe feet. Its front apron and legs are carved, and it retains small claw feet. However, the lines, like some of Gustav's earlier dining chairs, are essentially rectilinear in design. If one were to remove the carving on these and some of the earlier dining chairs, we would be close to the suggestions of a severe style as advocated by Albert Stickley when he returned from England in March of 1900, only six months after the introduction of this Morris chair.

Within a year, Gustav Stickley would drop the final "e" from his name and introduce his "New Furniture" in Grand Rapids. These new designs were forms without the carving, forms that would take him in a new direction. Upon this, he would formulate a new set of principles, ones that were based in reform and simplicity.

During the last quarter of the nineteenth century, acceptance of the Arts & Crafts movement had been slow. The ideas proposed by John Ruskin and William Morris were accepted by the furniture companies, but they were not put into practice by the larger manufacturers. The public at large had not accepted them any more than the aristocracy had in England. The movement did not gain popularity with the masses in America or Europe until the twentieth century. As one thumbs through issues of the English furniture trade journals, it seems that they, like the American trade press, freely quoted or praised figures like Morris or Ruskin, but the work rarely seems to have translated into products for the larger public until the end of the century. England accepted the "plain and severe" styles more quickly than America, but not as quickly as one might imagine.

As the turn of the century approached, Gustav and Albert Stickley seemed to be working in tandem toward some of the same forms in design based on English Arts & Crafts models. Albert was familiar with the English design aesthetic, and the two brothers must have discussed the new English concepts in conjunction with the historical styles they had been producing. Later, Gustav would write in the *Craftsman* that he had produced "adaptations of the historic styles, but always under silent protest."[63]

Gustav and Albert were not alone in their thoughts. Others began to produce objects for public consumption based on Arts & Crafts ideals. By 1899, the *International Studio* and *Dekorative Kunst* had published in America the English and Scottish Arts & Crafts work of Baillie Scott, C. R. Ashbee, C. F. A. Voysey, A. H. Mackmurdo, and Charles Rennie Mackintosh. The result was that the Arts & Crafts aesthetic made an impact on America by following British models. It flourished in Arts & Crafts societies that were being set up in cities in America in 1898. Joseph P. McHugh had already made his mark in the style at his Popular Shop in New York much earlier as had others.[64] Notice of his work appeared in November of 1899 in the *Furniture World* as well as in the *International Studio,* well in advance of any of the Stickley innovations. McHugh's Arts & Crafts furniture had been in development, as had other forms, since 1895. Significantly, in 1900, the World's Fair in Paris would introduce the world to a host of new ideas that would clearly inspire Gustav Stickley and others to experiment further. Thus, the acceptance of the Arts & Crafts ideals was to be part of the new century based on the Victorian principles of reform of one's environment, and all the Stickley brothers would play an integral part.

Opposite:
Gustav Stickley rectilinear, shoe-footed Morris chair, model 2316, the *Furniture World*, July 27, 1899.

63. Gustav Stickley, "Thoughts," *Craftsman*, 42.

64. See Wendy Kaplan, *The Art That is Life*, 56, 185, for a brief description of his impact (185) and for the establishment of various American Arts & Crafts societies in Boston, New York, and other American cities following British models (56).

IT FITS THE SITTER

2316

The lines of the back of MORRIS CHAIR No. 2316 conform so nicely to the form of the sitter that the highest degree of comfort is assured. It is one of our handsomest chairs, and is a rapid seller.

*

See it.
Buy it.

GUSTAVE STICKLEY CO.,
SYRACUSE, N. Y.

Gustav and Albert's Contributions

**Gustav Stickley living room of Craftsman House
number X, the _Craftsman_, October 1904.**

I n 1900, both Gustav and Albert Stickley made their
stylistic voices heard among a hoard of others clam-
oring in the wake of the Exposition Universelle held
in Paris. Gustav Stickley introduced his "New
Furniture," and Albert Stickley introduced both
English Arts & Crafts and Art Nouveau pieces into his
existing lines. However, both continued to market their
safe, conventional designs well into the new century. The
brothers' initial experiments, both innovative and derivative, received attention and approval from the American
public and trade press. In the meantime, Charles, Leopold,
and John George began to move in new directions. As
John Towse noted, it would not be until the end of the first
decade before all the Stickley brothers were "engaged in the
manufacture of mission and Arts & Crafts furniture."
Thus, we return first to Gustav and Albert for a microcosm
of the furniture industry.

The experimentation exhibited by the Stickley brothers
increased dramatically worldwide after the exposition in
Paris. It brought many of the European design forms to
gether under one roof. Numerous furniture manufacturers

from throughout the United States attended the fair. Albert attended prior to its opening, while others read about the innovations published in the national and international art and trade journals. Countless new forms were being born in the wake of the exposition. The Stickley brothers, along with others, were caught up in the excitement.

GUSTAV STICKLEY'S TRANSFORMATION

Gustav Stickley's transformation was quick and decisive. Before 1900, he was a little-known player in the furniture industry. Although his designs after his 1895 and 1896 visits to Europe represented both creativity and experimentation, these designs only demonstrated the current, mediocre fashion. There was nothing with true distinction. At first glance, there seems very little to warrant the sudden innovative explosion that drove him and his work from 1900 to 1916. Yet, in a matter of a few years, he would rise from obscurity to become the leader of the American Arts & Crafts movement.

Albert had already demonstrated his prowess in venture taking and clearly articulated his business objectives and philosophy in England. He had become a major manufacturer in the "furniture city" and had taken on a European experiment with several Grand Rapids furniture makers, an experiment that prospered. Because of his frequent trips abroad, Albert understood the English and European tastes. Perhaps, in some small way, the link between Gustav and Albert helped stimulate Gustav's going in new directions.

Gustav Stickley premiered his new work in Grand Rapids during the summer exposition of 1900. For the furniture world, it was a radical display. He wrote eloquently of his own transformation toward these latest forms:

> In making preparations for my new departure, I found others setting out with objects similar to my own. This was to be expected, since the germs of revolution never concentrate in a single locality or a single brain. Reform was in the air, seeking soils favorable to its development. . . . I further resolved that I would never again be an imitator, and I set my face toward absolute radicalism. At that time, the revulsion toward simplicity created in America the so-called Dutch, Tyrolean peasant, and Mission styles; while from the other side of the Atlantic ripples of influence reached us: from France, Belgium, and from Japan as misunderstood by the Europeans.[1]

As Gustav struggled with the creation of his latest objects, he was fully aware of the influences he was under and that others were working in the same directions following similar influences. He discussed his earlier work where "in obedience to the public demand, I produced in my workshops adaptations of the historic styles, but always under silent protest: my opposition developing, as I believe, out of a course of reading, largely from Ruskin and Emerson, which I followed in my early youth."[2] His goal was to create an American "democratic art" based on simple structure.

David Cathers has traced Gustav Stickley's chronological development and transformation in

1. Gustav Stickley, "Thoughts," *Craftsman*, October 1904, 44.

2. Ibid., 42.

Opposite: Advertisement for "New Furniture from the workshop of Gustave Stickley," the *Furniture World*, October 25, 1900.

No. 10

No. 5½

NEW FURNITURE

from the workshop of

GUSTAVE STICKLEY, CABINET MAKER,

SYRACUSE, N. Y.

No. 1

No. 26

Tobey advertisement for The New Furniture by Gustave Stickley, the *House Beautiful*, October 1900.

his ongoing analysis of Gustav's work and ideas. His analysis is one of the best and most comprehensive of the variations in Gustav's work. He has broken down the development of his style into four fairly distinct evolutionary periods: the experimental period, 1898–1900; the Craftsman period, 1900–1904; the mature production period, 1904–1910; and the final production period, 1910–1916.[3] Thus, except where specifically noted, we have followed Cathers' lead in the subsequent passages.

Stickley indicated that he began experimenting with his "new furniture" as early as 1898 and that over the next two years he struggled "over the main problems of design, construction and finishing."[4] In 1900, he went public with the results. In the spring, Towse noted that since March, Gustav Stickley's sales had dropped and that he would produce "a line of cheap, medium and fine dining chairs" for the summer season.[5] He noted:

> There will be somewhat of a departure from the goods as now manufactured. New furniture and new finishes will be shown the trade in July entirely different from work hitherto produced. The main feature of the forthcoming production will be small pieces, which may be properly termed novelties. There will also be shown the usual line of fancy rockers, in unique and original creations.[6]

By the summer of 1900, advertisements began to appear in various trade journals announcing that Gustav would be at the July exposition in Grand Rapids with Leopold Stickley, representing his newest line of furniture.[7] In spite of the favorable reviews Gustav received for his new "novelties," the *Furniture World* continued to run his advertisement with the conventional 2316 Morris Chair. He ran more than forty-one, quarter-page inside-cover advertisements in less than a year for this particular chair. It was December before the advertisements in this trade journal began to feature four examples of the new line in the same prominent position.

David Cathers and Sharon Darling have thoroughly explained the events following the summer exposition in Grand Rapids. Gustav Stickley arranged with George F. Clingman, head designer for the Tobey Furniture Company, to distribute his new furniture. In October, an advertisement under the Tobey label appeared in the *Chicago Tribune* as part of an extensive advertising campaign to exploit the "New Furniture." According to the advertisement, the furniture belonged to a "school of design almost unknown in this country but understood and in great esteem in Europe . . ." Its model was found in the Glasgow school of design and the design of the late William Morris. The advertisement announced "Furniture as an Educator" and indicated that "it was a departure from all established styles, a casting off of the shackles of the past—the only influence being the present."[8] Other advertisements for the New Furniture and an illustrated article about it appeared in the October through December issues of the *House Beautiful*. However, by October, the name of one furniture finish was changed from "Austrian" to "weathered oak," and Clingman added a trademark label of his own.[9] According to Darling, in a letter to Leopold Stickley in 1911, Clingman claimed to be the originator of Mission furniture and asserted that he had given Gustav the ideas

3. Gustav Stickley, "Craftsman Furniture," 1912 in David Cathers, *Furniture of the American Arts & Crafts Movement: Furniture Made by Gustav Stickley, L. & J. G. Stickley and the Roycroft Shop*, revised edition (Philmont, NY: Turn of the Century Editions, 1996), 44.

4. Ibid., 44.

5. John Towse, "On the Road," *Furniture World*, 17 May 1900, 5.

6. Ibid.

7. *American Cabinet Maker and Upholsterer*, 30 June 1900 in Cathers, *Furniture*, 62,

8. Cathers, *Furniture*, 44-47, 62. For the advertisement and his comments on the period (44-47). Also see his note (62). The most comprehensive discussion of the Tobey and Stickley relationship may be found in Sharon Darling, *Chicago Furniture: Art, Craft, & Industry 1833–1983* (New York: W. W. Norton & Company, 1984), 232-247.

9. The Tattler, "Tattle of the Trade," the *Furniture Journal*, 10 October 1900, 9.

10. Darling, *Chicago*, 233.

11. David Cathers, "Gustav Stickley's 1900 Line," *Style 1900*, November 2001, 19.

12. Darling suggests that Leopold Stickley may have finished the contract and Cathers points to such evidence as the drawings found in the basement of the L. & J. G. Stickley factory by Donald Davidoff, which offer evidence of dealings by L. & J. G. with Tobey and other firms. Further evidence in an unpublished catalog of Tobey's Russmore Furniture showing early Onondaga Shops work suggests the same. However, evidence as to finishing the contract remains, as Cathers notes, "inconclusive."

13. Cathers, "Gustav Stickley's 1900 Line," 19.

for his next phase of design. Tobey would continue to produce Arts & Crafts furniture and make a major advertising campaign based on its introduction.

Darling indicates that, in the final analysis, "Tobey Furniture Company was one of the first American retailers to aggressively market factory-made Arts & Crafts furniture using modern advertising techniques and brand-name identification."[10] Cathers concludes that "Tobey's well-coordinated, wide-reaching market efforts and ability to make effective use of modern mass communications played an important role in helping Stickley's new furniture achieve almost immediate popularity."[11]

The success of the New Furniture was not solely due to Tobey's creative marketing. As Cathers points out, the new line was "good furniture" and well designed. The designs were combined with the new ideas and influences that were surfacing throughout the decorative arts and coming together at the beginning of the new century. This was Gustav Stickley's attempt, with the aid of Tobey, to stake his claim as a part of the new international movement, and he was successful. With the introduction of the line, Gustav's standing in the trade grew. It was the beginning of the Stickley brothers' new voice. They were now members and soon to be leaders of a much larger international movement.

By the end of the year, both Tobey and Stickley had issued strikingly similar catalogs for the New Furniture. Gustav had broken off the deal with Tobey to produce the line, and the debate continues as to who canceled the Tobey contract.[12] The "novelties" that appeared in Gustav's catalog (and Tobey's as well) were derivative and owe homage to Stickley's earlier designs and methodology. Cathers has recently pointed again to these connections in his own analysis of the early experimental forms.[13] It is clear that Gustav utilized many of the forms that he had used before. Cathers points specifically to a number of possible sources: his villa or Japanese bamboo suite from 1897; colonial forms from his

Celandine circular tea table, model 27 from The New Furniture line, 1900. Detail of carved and incised celandine poppy motif from the tabletop.

Left: Cover of the catalog of New Furniture from the Shop of the Tobey Furniture Company.

Below: Pages 22 and 23 illustrate Gustav Stickley's Bungalow Settee, Bungalow Rocker, and Bungalow Library Chair from the same catalog.

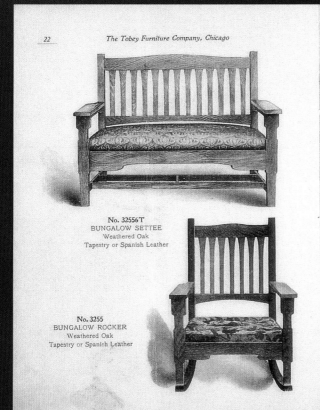

22   *The Tobey Furniture Company, Chicago*

The Tobey Furniture Company, Chicago   23

No. 32556 T
BUNGALOW SETTEE
Weathered Oak
Tapestry or Spanish Leather

No. 3255
BUNGALOW ROCKER
Weathered Oak
Tapestry or Spanish Leather

No. 32556
BUNGALOW LIBRARY CHAIR
Weathered Oak   Tapestry or Leather

Left: Detail of a magazine rack and a tabourette from the Villa suite, the *Upholsterer,* March 1897.

Below: Damascus Plant Stand with Grueby tile top, model 9 from the New Furniture line, 1900.

Right: Gustav Stickley Chalet Magazine Cabinet, model 500, about 1900. This stand was model 3500 in the Tobey catalog.

Stickley and Simonds years; European Art Nouveau ideas gleaned from various journals; Charles Rohlfs, and finally various medieval forms. At least two of the forms (the magazine stand and two small tabourets) that appear in the villa suite can be linked to the forms that appear in Gustav's New Furniture.

While Cathers is correct about the sources, the designs with their associated names evoke an international flavor that was clearly Stickley's doing, not Tobey's. Gustav had used the technique previously, selecting names like Lenox to evoke an identity with American Shaker furniture when he was in partnership with Simonds. For example, in the first New Furniture catalog, plant stands with Grueby tile tops appear with names like Bombay, Mikado, and Damascus—which conjure images of the Near and Far East—to others, such as Cottage Manor or Morris that evoke the English countryside. The tabourets use flower motifs, carved in the Nancy style, with names like Lotos, Foxglove, and even Sunflower. Other pieces called Tom Jones and Bellworth are definitely reminiscent of English themes. There is even one pedestal that is titled Venetian. Such names were not happenstance but were as intentional as the Nantucket and Lenox chairs of Gustav's Stickley and Simonds years. The selection of a name to evoke a theme for a furniture line had been used before. The intention was to make it international and link it with the World's Fair and spirit of the new century. These designs are not Arts & Crafts in the English sense but are experimental.

Here, for the first time, Gustav experimented with structure as ornament. Through-tenons pierce the legs of stands, and carving is minimal. Often, low-relief carving was used to evoke the form of the whole work and the name of the piece. They were also Gustav's attempt to make the movement work on a larger scale, one more palatable to an American audience. However, the result was not exactly what Gustav envisioned, and he prepared to push his designs in other directions. At the end of 1900, he rented a showroom space with room for expansion at the Crouse Stables in Syracuse. Eventually, this would become the first Craftsman Building and house the initial phases of his campaign for an Arts & Crafts way of living.[14] It would be the first step in the direction of creating an American style of design based on structure.

During the next five years, Gustav Stickley would create what he felt was the basic American expression of design and bring it to its essential form. The years between 1900 and 1903 were critical to the development of the structural forms that became fundamental to his approach and created the essence of its style. It is also clear that others played a role in the development of his designs. According to David Cathers, LaMont A. Warner, who worked for Gustav Stickley between 1900 and 1906, may have played an important role in the designs that were done during Gustav's early years. A total picture of the tangled web that Cathers unfolds would be difficult to play out here. Likewise, it would be impossible within these few pages to plunge into the depth of design innovations from these years. Cathers and others have given a more-than-adequate survey of each of the transformations and have given copious examples of the influences of others, so we will limit ourselves to some basic observations.[15]

True to his promise of structural forms, Gustav Stickley stripped away all ornament that was not essential. Carving was no longer essential to the form and virtually disappeared from his work.

14. *American Cabinet Maker and Upholsterer* (22 December 1900) in Cathers, *Furniture,* 16. Also see Mary Ann Smith, *Gustave Stickley: The Craftsman* (Mineola, NY: Dover Publications, 1983), 24-26 for a discussion of the new showroom and its history. Also see in *Collected Works of Gustav Stickley* (Philmont, NY: Turn of the Century Editions, 1981), 19-20 for interior illustrations of the newly renovated building.

15. Cathers, *Furniture,* 44-64 for an excellent, concise treatment of the periods. Also, one may trace the evolution through his survey and commentary on the various forms, 107-239. What follows in my own survey closely follows the Cathers' commentary except where specifically noted.

This was perhaps best demonstrated in his earliest work from 1901 and 1902, first exemplified in his *Chips from the Workshop*, printed in June of 1901, and in copies of the *Craftsman,* which began publication in October of that year. These early forms are characterized by the extensive use of obvious structural units such as the keyed, through-tenon, or butterfly joints, the purpose of which is both decorative and functional. Gustav pointed out, "The only decoration that seems in keeping with simple structural forms lies in the emphasizing of certain features of the construction, such as the mortise, tenon, key, and dovetail." [16]

16. Gustav Stickley, *Chips*, 1906 in *Collected Works*, 17.

The forms are massive and linear but are frequently softened by the curves of the supporting members, rounded tops, and pointed "rabbit ears" on settles and chairs. Arches that appear Gothic or medieval form the top mullions of bookcases or become part of the structural motifs on the backs of settles and chairs. Chamfered backs are common on the sideboards and bookcases. The trumpeted slats, as seen on the bungalow chairs of the New Furniture, become straight, and lines tend toward the linear. Pyramidal tops appear on the through-posts of the arms on some chairs, and the through-tenon is common, with or without a key, on rails and stretchers. The early pulls are often a mixture of metal and wooden knobs. The earliest metalwork was simple brass and iron-beveled plates. Some of the early butterfly plates with their pyramidal pulls and the oversized wooden knobs appear quite massive in proportion. The effect makes a piece appear to be designed to "endure." Gustav Stickley best described the purpose of his new designs:

17. Ibid., 19.

18. Cathers, *Furniture*, 106.

> The Craftsman furniture is designed solely for use and comfort and durability, and the beauty that is peculiarly its own arises from the directness with which it meets these requirements as well as from the structural integrity of the design itself. Clumsiness and crudity are not and never have been a part of my idea. While a massive simplicity is the leading characteristic of the style, each piece is finely proportioned and as carefully finished as the work of the old Colonial cabinet-makers, and is as well-fitted to endure. [17]

Gustav's notes on "comfort and durability," as well as "beauty" in defense against "crudity," are two of the cornerstones against the onslaught of attacks on American Arts & Crafts furniture design. For Gustav Stickley, being "plain" was not the same as being "crude." [18]

The furniture line produced after 1901 was extensive compared to the small number of chairs and other items that he had

Gustav Stickley card table with faceted wooden pulls, stretchers mortised through the legs and a keyed-through tenon center stretcher, model 447, about 1902.

Opposite: Gustav Stickley oak sideboard featuring cabinet doors with butterfly keys, pyramidal pulls and exposed keyed tenons, model 901, about 1901.

produced before then. Gustav retained a few items in his repertoire from the New Furniture line, including the Bungalow Table, the Chalet Desk, the Spanish Arm Chair and the Venetian Pedestal. In most cases, he simply dropped the name and retained the numbers of the old pieces. By the end of 1902, he had produced a complete line of furnishings for every room in the home. United Crafts, as Gustav's company was now called, even exhibited at the Mechanic's Fair in Boston a complete living room, bedroom, dining room and office, all furnished by items from his Eastwood Factory." [19]

In the meantime, Gustav assertively marketed his products through his own publication, the *Craftsman*. In October of 1901, he began to publish a monthly periodical that not only informed the Arts & Crafts community of what his company offered, but also espoused the philosophy of the new movement through the words and works of others. He added editorial facilities to his Craftsman Building. In November of 1902, John Towse could not find Stickley at the plant because

19. *Collected Works*, 34-35 for illustrations of the exhibit.

Left:
Gustav Stickley drop front desk with chamfered sides, model 518, about 1902.

Above:
Gustav Stickley "Rabbit Ear" oak settle with tapering posts and gothic arches incorporated into the slat design of the back and sides, model 165, about 1902.

Opposite, right:
Gustav oak server with pyramidal "butterfly" wrought-iron pulls, about 1901.

he was busy "at his editorial desk of the *Craftsman*." According to Towse, "[h]e (Gustav) is working hard to build up the magazine. The offices of this publication are furnished with furniture of the United Crafts, and are not only handsome but extremely unique. . . . Stickley is carrying out a great scheme in connection with his manufacturing business and the magazine."[20] Gustav clarified the so-called scheme in the first few issues. After dedicating the first issue to William Morris, "one of the strongest Anglo-Saxon heroes of the nineteenth century," and the second to John Ruskin, "whose exaltation, or rather, divine madness" had awakened Gustav's "ambitions" in his early youth, he turned to practical matters.[21] The "monograph" was to be turned into a periodical that would:

> Publish any writing which might increase public respect for honest, intelligent labor; advance the cause of civic improvement; diffuse a critical knowledge of modern art, as shown in its most characteristic examples chosen from the fine, decorative, or industrial divisions; advocate the 'integral education,' or in other words, the simultaneous training of hand and brain; and thus help to make the workshop an adjunct of the school.[22]

Even given Gustav's supposedly noble and objective intentions, he was not above assembling "certain objects of craftsmanship and small decorative schemes which correspond more or less closely

20. Towse, "On the Road," *Furniture World*, 27 November 1902, 7.

21. Gustav Stickley, "Thoughts," *Craftsman*, October 1904, 56.

22. Ibid., 57.

Group of the *Craftsman* maga-zines.

23. Ibid., 57-58.

24. Cathers, *Furniture*, 49.

to my ideas. Other than in the pieces of cabinet-making, which are the products of my own work-shops, I have sought to choose typical, or else very pleasing examples of foreign contemporary work."[23] As Gustav marketed his merchandise through the *Craftsman*, he actively sought other venues as well. In 1901, both Gustav and Albert displayed their furniture at the Pan American Exposition in Buffalo. For Gustav, it would be the first national exposure for the new line created by United Crafts.

During 1902, Gustav's furniture continued to evolve and mature. Cathers briefly summarized the changes:

> In 1902, Stickley's furniture design became more assured. It grew increasingly rectilinear and severe, with the modest curves and moldings giving way to robust geometrical forms. In 1903, these designs were replaced by lighter pieces as the Craftsman period drew to a close.[24]

The year of 1903 was a watershed for Gustav with a shift to lighter forms—a shift that would set a pattern or tone for the rest of his line through its maturity. His forms would remain structurally oriented but would lose their massive quality. It was a period of standardization for his work.

The trend toward lighter forms was influenced by a number of events that occurred during 1903. In 1902, Irene Sargent, editor of the *Craftsman*, had toured Europe, more than likely to gather

Dining room from 1903 exhibition at the Craftsman Building, Syracuse, NY, the *Craftsman*, May 1903.

information and prepare the way for Gustav's subsequent trip in late 1902 and early 1903. Gustav's journey was planned as a buying and research trip for a major exhibition he was arranging for the Craftsman Building in Syracuse in March and April of 1903. He purchased works by C. F. A. Voysey and objects from the London firm of J. S. Henry, to name a few. During 1903, many of these purchases appeared at one time or another in the *Craftsman*. Many of the design elements seen in these pieces, such as overhanging tops and inlays, would be reflected in the work of Stickley's new designer, Harvey Ellis of Rochester, New York.[25]

Stickley hired Ellis in the spring of 1903, and he became a major design influence on Stickley, both as an architect and a furniture designer. In the year to come, Ellis would design interiors and exteriors of homes for Stickley. Ellis would fill these homes with his lighter, more sophisticated furniture—structurally simple and elegantly decorated with inlay. These exquisite new furniture designs with intricate, inlaid surfaces became a standard for 1903.

In July of 1903, Ellis's exteriors, interiors, and new inlay designs were published in the *Craftsman*. By January of 1904, his furniture appeared in the trade journals. Ellis died in January of 1904 and was buried in an unmarked grave in Syracuse. Although Ellis's inlay designs were limited and short-lived, his graceful yet structural style had a major impact on the rest of Stickley's work.

25. Cathers, *Furniture*, 38.

26. Cathers' most recent observations on Ellis and the influences of Gustav Stickley's 1903 trip to England are persuasive. As Cathers correctly observes, there are multiple influences at play in all of Stickley's design choices. "Mr. Stickley Goes to London," presentation at the 2002 Arts & Crafts Conference, Grove Park Inn, Asheville, NC, February 2002.

His importance lies not so much in the introduction of inlay to the furniture but in the change of the structural form. As Cathers points out, such alterations clearly related to the work and style of Voysey and multiple other influences that came to bear on Ellis in that year.[26] The chairs designed by Ellis are more buoyant, with graceful, curved seat rails and taller, thinner, slatted backs. Some chairs have shoe feet that accent the characteristic arched rails. Beyond these arches, found also on the china cabinets and bookcases, we find overhanging tops and less emphasis on the hardware except when accented by the inlay. The near-perfect harmony evident in all of Ellis's easily identifiable design work is in marked contrast to the heavier work of the earlier period. The design marks a move in a new direction.

At the end of 1903, Gustav made a shift toward lighter structural forms, and 1904 marked the initial stages of the formulation of his Craftsman empire. At the first of the year, he introduced the Craftsman Home Builders Club. The *Craftsman* ran a series of designs for a variety of homes, mostly geared toward middle-class Americans who wanted to live the Arts & Crafts lifestyle. These new homes, inspired by Harvey Ellis's designs for the *Craftsman*, also bear Gustav's own imprint, developed during the reconstruction of his own

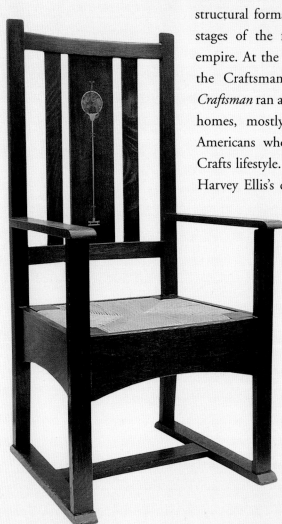

Left: Gustav Stickley shoe foot inlaid armchair, attributed to Harvey Ellis, about 1903–1904.

Right: Inlaid oak piano and bench designed by Harvey Ellis about 1903. Produced for the interior of Gustav Stickley's house at 438 Columbus Avenue, Syracuse, NY.

Overleaf: Inlaid oak settle designed by Harvey Ellis or LaMont A. Warner for Gustav Stickley, about 1903. This settle is based on a design by M. H. Baillie Scott, produced by John P. Whited of the Pyghtle Works in Bedford, England in 1901.

Gustav Stickley dining room interior designed by Harvey Ellis and published in the *Craftsman*, November 1905.

home in Syracuse after a fire had destroyed the interior. A description of the redesigned interior appeared in the February 1903 issue in an article by Samuel Howe.[27] Stickley almost immediately hired Ernest G. W. Dietrich as an architect to design the first Craftsman home to be published in the *Craftsman* in May of 1903.[28] In subsequent months, Ellis's designs for homes and their interiors filled the pages of the *Craftsman*. The designs for these usually small, middle-class homes are centered around a large living space that contains a hearth around which the family can gather. A dining room, library, and kitchen occupy the first floor, with bedrooms on the second floor. These homes were based on Gustav's concept of simplicity and usually feature built-in bookcases and window seats. From 1904 on, the homes became a regular feature of the *Craftsman* and were essential to establishing the Arts & Crafts lifestyle.

After a halfhearted attempt at creating a new name for his company via a contest in the *Craftsman*, Gustav, by the end of 1903, changed the name of United Crafts to Craftsman Workshops. By 1905, he applied for and was granted copyright for the registered name "Craftsman" as his trademark, along with the joiner's compass and his familiar logo, "Als ik Kan" (Flemish for "As I Can"). Gustav became obsessed with stopping those who would "imitate" his

27. Samuel Howe, "A Visit to the House of Mr. Stickley," *Craftsman*, February 1903, 166-169.

28. See Mary Ann Smith, *Gustav Stickley*, 55-69 for her description of Dietrich and Ellis's role in the development of the Craftsman houses.

Opposite: Detail of the scenic inlay of copper, pewter, and exotic woods from the settle designed by Harvey Ellis or LaMont A. Warner.

Overleaf: Exterior of Craftsman House number X, the *Craftsman*, October 1904.

work. This sensitivity was revealed in June of 1904 in an article in the *Craftsman*. It marked the beginning of a long battle that ended in a 1910 civil suit in the United States Circuit Court in Pittsburgh, Pennsylvania, against the Kaufmann brothers and their department store. Stickley charged the brothers with trademark infringement and accused them of unfair competition—selling furniture that directly imitated his new style. He attempted to claim the rights to the name "Craftsman" and to any work that was similar in style to his own.[29] The suit was finally dismissed in March 1911. It was a losing battle because between 1904 and 1905, the Arts & Crafts movement and Mission furniture had become national trends.

29. See Michael E. Clark and Jill Thomas-Clark, "Gustav vs. Kaufmann Brothers," *Style 1900*, February 1997, 45-47 for a full account of the court case and shop mark argument.

Living room showing a clock, a buffet, and wainscoating designed by Professor Maximilian Sänger that were part of the German exhibition at the Louisiana Purchase Exposition, St. Louis, 1904; the *Craftsman*, August 1904.

In the summer of 1904, Gustav attended the exposition in St. Louis and later wrote two articles for the *Craftsman* that articulated not only his opinion of the exposition but also his thoughts on the unity of design and purpose. The articles reflect the evolution of his style and foreshadow much of what was to come. In them, Gustav discusses imitation, structure and decoration of objects and rooms, and the relationship of his design to an American style.

The first article appeared in the August issue. In it, Gustav criticized the exposition because it "fails to attain its chief purpose; that is: it does not adequately represent the nations participating in it, or mark a definite point in the world's progress in the arts and sciences, in inventions and manufactures." To illustrate his point, he called attention to the Japanese exhibit and one of the American exhibits. He indicated that the Japanese exhibit had "chosen to present what their artists and craftsmen have derived from European and American influences, and what, in imitating, they have half comprehended; thus, corrupting and debasing the work of their own hands."[30] He also criticized one unidentified American exhibition that was "composed entirely of objects in the French historic styles." To him, they were like "the Japanese ware copied from Western models, they are without spirit or meaning. They have no reason for existence, since they were not, like their originals, created to serve some definite end."[31] This criticism is directly linked to Gustav's concept that each nation has its own style that must be developed on its own and reflect the national character. According to Gustav, the rationale behind these imitations was "the scourge of commercialism." He

30. Ibid., 492.

31. Ibid.

felt that these "manufacturers found it easier and more profitable to imitate a known quantity rather than come up with their own ideas based on the needs, manners and customs of a new and strongly individual people."[32] His attack against those that would imitate the work of others echoed his complaints against those that imitated his own work.

32. Ibid.

Gustav found one exhibit to be of particular merit—the North German exhibit. He was not alone in his praise for it. Most furniture dealers, retailers, and critics who visited the fair applauded its design and execution. However, they felt that the high-quality, detailed handwork made its commercial production impractical. One member of the "International Jury of Awards" noted:

The cost of the furniture in one of the German furnished rooms—the furniture alone, not the fixed furniture or interior work of the room, which would have been quite necessary, by the way, to have preserved the excellent effect—with that of one of the American booths, both being made of oak, and on somewhat similar lines, the German being the New Art, as they term it, and the American the Arts & Crafts, and the German furniture, piece for piece, was more than double the cost of the American, and it certainly individually did not excel in construction, material, intarsia or inlay work, or in artistic quality, away from its environments.[33]

Scheme for a fireplace: the copper hood adapted from a design of Professor J. M. Olbrich, shown at the German exhibition, St. Louis, 1904; the *Craftsman*, October 1904.

The American booth cited was the gold-medal-winning Arts & Crafts exhibit of Albert Stickley. The critic conceded a pivotal concept of the German exhibit—the interior was integral to the display and was equally as important as the furniture. Much of the exhibit relied on built-in settings and the total environment, which would have greatly interested Gustav in relation to the designs for his new Craftsman Homes, which also relied heavily on a total unified design concept.

When Gustav reviewed the German exhibit in an article for the *Craftsman*, he admired the furniture and the execution of the rooms. In his analysis, he emphasized the importance of space in the design of the whole. He noted "the fine utilization of space which is largely responsible for the effect of cohesiveness and unity." He found that though the design showed "a deep study of historic styles," it had "no savor of the encyclopaedia or the student's drawing book." He admired "in this architectural composition the time-honored principles of the arch, the colonnade, the inclined roof

33. "Judging the Furniture at the World's Fair," *Grand Rapids Furniture Record*, August 1904, 497.

and the open rafters joined together in a harmony which sings." Here he could easily be describing one of his own Craftsman Home interiors. More specifically, he found favor with "a private residence" designed by Professor Leo Nachtlicht of Berlin. Gustav observed that, "all monumental features are eliminated, as they should be, in domestic architecture; both construction and ornament evidencing a freedom and flexibility which are wanting in the historic styles" because the room had been adapted to "homes of modern citizens of the world." He liked the color and the lines of the objects that "remain as a tribute offered by the new art to the principle of simplicity."[34] A few pages later, he admired that "the ceilings of these houses were always low." In one room, he attacked the use of tacked-on pewter because it was only "applied to the surface" and not inlaid into it. Gustav's final judgement was that the whole display was "one of simplicity and symmetry, which are complementary forces—so much more difficult to employ than a superfluity."[35]

By October of 1904, Gustav Stickley made his appeal for America and its "democratic art" and defined the American style as primarily structural. To support that plea, he looked to the structural simplicity of the German exhibition and blended his own work with that of the Germans. He found harmony between the structural elements of the German setting and its objects. Therefore, in the October issue of the *Craftsman*, there appears a Gustav Stickley interior inspired by an interior from the German exhibit by Professor Max Sänger of Karlsruhe. Gustav also found inspiration in the work of other designers at the fair. For example, in one composite design illustration he adapts a setting by the Viennese Herr Hoffman to include a Harvey Ellis chair sitting at a Hoffman built-in desk.

The following year marked the beginning of another shift in Gustav's focus. In addition to a continuing trend toward lighter forms, he began to solidify and standardize his designs. According to Cathers, in 1905 Gustav "developed a line of tables and chairs using spindle construction."[36] The inspiration for this popular line is unclear. Cathers suggests that it might have developed from Frank Lloyd Wright's interior designs for the Darwin Martin House in Buffalo or just as a wise marketing move to continue the creation of the new lighter work that the public was demanding. In either case, it was probably one of the more significant developments during the

Design by Gustav Stickley for a treatment of a wainscoating adapted from an interior by Professor Maximilian Sänger as seen on page 74; the *Craftsman*, October 1904.

34. Gustav Stickley, "The German Exhibit at the Louisiana Purchase Exposition," *Craftsman*, August 1904, 501.

35. Ibid., 506.

36. Cathers, *Furniture*, 59.

years between 1905 and 1910. Other changes appeared in his line during these years. Cathers points to the changes in the hardware: "the V-shaped pull first used in 1904, the flattened V-shape, introduced the same year and made in three sizes, and oversized round pulls which appeared on built-ins in the *Craftsman* as early as 1908 but were not used on furniture until about 1910."[37] Other minor changes occurred, but most seemed to be focused on design standardization and formulation. It seemed that by 1910, Gustav had perfected his design work. By 1912, he pointed out, "Most of my furniture was so carefully designed and well-proportioned in the first place, that even I with my advanced experience cannot improve upon it."[38]

Concurrently, other administrative changes were taking place. In April of 1905, Irene Sargent

37. Ibid.

38. Gustav Stickley, "Craftsman Furniture," 1912 in Cathers, *Furniture*, 60.

had resigned as editor of the *Craftsman*. According to Cleota Reed, Sargent explained in a letter to Henry Turner Bailey that "New departures are planned for the magazine which appear to me neither wise nor desirable, and my New England blood gives me sufficient obstinacy to resist them, even against my own interests."[39] The new departures were apparently theoretical as well as geographic. By the end of 1905, Gustav had sold his Craftsman Building in Syracuse, moved to New York City, and opened showrooms there. The move marked a shift in emphasis from small-city life to a more cosmopolitan, middle- to upper-middle-class focus for both Gustav and his enterprises.

By the end of the decade, Gustav had moved his family from Syracuse to Craftsman Farms in Morris Plains, New Jersey. He was now commuting to work at his offices in the city. As he approached the second decade of the new century, the Arts & Crafts movement in America had peaked and joined the mainstream. The initial stages of change began to occur just as Gustav planned more extensive alterations not only in his business but also in his planning for enriching the American way of life. These changes were constantly reflected by the new ideas and plans published in the *Craftsman*. During these years, he emphasized his expanding product line and what he considered to be the correct Arts & Crafts lifestyle.

As early as 1908, Gustav had begun to publish his plans for Craftsman Farms, his vision of a utopian community where young men would be educated in the appropriate lifestyle. Gustav's dream was to be built on a farm in New Jersey. After considerable planning and frequent articles

39. Letter from Irene Sargent to Henry Turner Bailey, February 1905, University of Oregon, Division of Special Collections and University Archives, AX 321. Originally quoted by Cleota Reed, *Courier* 30 (1995), 43.

Set of six oak and rush high-back spindle side chairs, model 384, about 1905, surrounding an oak Directors table, model 631½, about 1912.

on the progress of the construction of small bungalows and a clubhouse, the plan fizzled. In about 1914, the clubhouse simply became his new home. Other grand ideas that were planned did not come to fruition. He even sought ways to discover a national architectural style and improve American society through social planning.[40] All these ideas and plans for expansion came at a time when America was growing and turning to face a crisis in Europe. By 1913 Marilyn Fish points out:

> Stickley's personal and business responsibilities became truly oppressive. By then he was simultaneously coping with his family's move from Syracuse to Morris Plains; developing the architecture, landscape and school at Craftsman Farms; meeting the enormous expenses associated with the Craftsman Building; and struggling with declining public interest in his once-popular line of art furniture.[41]

During these years before his bankruptcy in 1916, Gustav continued to plan for a future that would not be.

Somewhere amid all the planning and stress on creating an Arts & Crafts lifestyle for others, it seems that Gustav's emphasis on the design of his furniture got lost. In his home at Craftsman Farms, he seemed to isolate himself. In the rustic log cabin clubhouse that became his home, he surrounded himself with many of

Gustav Stickley's log home at Craftsman Farms, Parsippany, NJ.

40. Fish, *The New Craftsman Index* (Lambertville, NJ: Arts & Crafts Quarterly Press, 1997), 18-20 for a concise development of Gustav's plans for the farms and various other projects, as told in the *Craftsman*.

41. Ibid., 21.

One end of the dining room in Stickley's home at Craftsman Farms, as it was published in the Craftsman, November 1911.

his earlier creations and accented it thematically the way he would have it. The living room contained his signature Eastwood chair, and the furnishings were strikingly simple throughout the home. Although some of the pieces were built for the home, the production pieces that furnished it were those of simple, honest construction. The dining room with its built-in corner cupboards and massive sideboard had tables that were surrounded by the simplest of his ladder-back, rush-seated chairs. Lost in this world, he was slow to adapt or oblivious to the changes that were occurring in the furniture industry.

As early as 1909, historical English revivals of Tudor, William and Mary, and Jacobean furniture had begun to be produced by other companies as they tried to adapt to America's desire for a change in tastes. The American and English Arts & Crafts styles began a slow decline in popularity and would run their course in the early 1920s. While other furniture companies, including some of his brothers', began to adapt, Gustav Stickley's firm did not react to the changes until at least 1913. His new designs were few, and they lacked the vitality and innovation seen earlier. Most of them were at odds with his Arts & Crafts philosophy that, a little over a decade before, had repudiated historical styles. By 1915, Gustav issued a new catalog that contained numerous examples of decorative items from other firms and only a few pieces of his own furniture. In that year the *Craftsman* advocated Gustav's Gumwood furniture and began to feature articles on historical styles.

Some articles praised the use of painted furniture to add color to the home, and others compared Sheraton furniture with that of Hepplewhite, Shearer, and Adam. A final judgement by the author came down in favor of Sheraton.[42]

By January of 1916, Gustav was defending good-quality imitations of historical styles with illustrations of his own designs.[43] However, in 1916, he claimed that the furniture he produced was still independent of any particular period or style and was based on good construction and finishes.[44] This was the year that he introduced the Chromewald line, which seemed to rely more on the finish than the design of the pieces. Nevertheless, the Chromewald line was different and innovative. Gustav claimed it was meant to blend with the various contemporary designs and was not based on a particular revival. However, Mary Anne Smith has suggested that "the new designs with their twined spindle legs seem to suggest American colonial and other historical models."[45] In May of 1916, Mary Fanton Roberts wrote an emotional introduction to the new line for the *Craftsman.* Nevertheless, the line could not save the failing company, and in March of 1915, Gustav

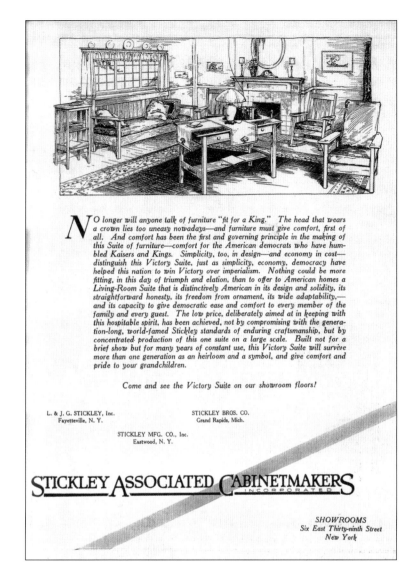

No longer will anyone talk of furniture "fit for a King." The head that wears a crown lies too uneasy nowadays—and furniture must give comfort, first of all. And comfort has been the first and governing principle in the making of this Suite of furniture—comfort for the American democrats who have humbled Kaisers and Kings. Simplicity, too, in design—and economy in cost—distinguish this Victory Suite, just as simplicity, economy, democracy have helped this nation to win Victory over imperialism. Nothing could be more fitting, in this day of triumph and elation, than to offer to American homes a Living-Room Suite that is distinctively American in its design and solidity, its straightforward honesty, its freedom from ornament, its wide adaptability,—and its capacity to give democratic ease and comfort to every member of the family and every guest. The low price, deliberately aimed at in keeping with this hospitable spirit, has been achieved, not by compromising with the generation-long, world-famed Stickley standards of enduring craftsmanship, but by concentrated production of this one suite on a large scale. Built not for a brief show but for many years of constant use, this Victory Suite will survive more than one generation as an heirloom and a symbol, and give comfort and pride to your grandchildren.

Come and see the Victory Suite on our showroom floors!

L. & J. G. STICKLEY, Inc.
Fayetteville, N. Y.

STICKLEY BROS. CO.
Grand Rapids, Mich.

STICKLEY MFG. CO., Inc.
Eastwood, N. Y.

STICKLEY ASSOCIATED CABINETMAKERS
INCORPORATED

SHOWROOMS
Six East Thirty-ninth Street
New York

Advertisement for Stickley Associated Cabinetmakers illustrating the Victory Suite, the *Furniture World,* November 28, 1918.

Stickley declared bankruptcy. Following the bankruptcy, the line became part of the amalgamation known as The Associated Cabinet Makers. Instigated by the L. & J. G. Stickley Company, the new company operated between 1917 and 1918 and consisted of three of the Stickley brothers' companies joined together (Gustav's, Leopold and John George's, and Albert's). Thus, it was Leopold, John George, and Albert who came to Gustav's aid in a time of need. In less than a year, Gustav unofficially retired from the new company, and the other brothers continued to confront the struggles of post-war America. However, two Stickley companies were up to facing the challenge of a post–Arts & Crafts world. Leopold, John George, and Albert, as furniture makers, continued to adapt to the new environment, while Gustav went into retirement in Syracuse.

42. See James Thomson, "The Intricate Elegance of Sheraton Art," *Craftsman,* May 1915, 183-189.

43. See Gustav Stickley, "The Ethics of Home Furnishings," *Craftsman,* January 1916, 412-420.

44. See Gustav Stickley, "Furniture Based Upon Good Craftsmanship," *Craftsman,* February 1916, 531-538.

45. Smith, *Gustav Stickley,* 156.

ALBERT STICKLEY: EVERYTHING ENGLISH

Whereas Gustav Stickley grew from a nonentity at the turn of the century, Albert Stickley, a national and international leader in the furniture industry, was already firmly established in the highly visible Grand Rapids environment. Beginning in 1896, Albert established himself abroad with his own enterprise. Various trade journals and Ellis Island ships' manifests indicate that after that date he made almost yearly trips abroad. For example, in 1900 one member of the trade press quoted a modest John Widdicomb as saying that it "was such men as the Berkeys, Slighs, Gay, Stickley, Luce, MacBride and others, and without boasting I can include Widdicomb, who made the furniture industry in Grand Rapids."[46] In the same issue of the *American Cabinet Maker and Upholsterer*, Stickley Brothers was listed as one of the companies authorized to use the newly issued "Made in Grand Rapids" label. It was a "seal of approval" used by members of the Grand Rapids Furniture Manufacturers Association, a group made up of the best of the Grand Rapids companies. According to Christian Carron, "Its appearance on a piece of furniture was meant as an assurance of quality and an authentication that the piece originated from Grand Rapids, Michigan."[47] Although the English critics might have condemned the Grand Rapids manufacturers for their "machine made" goods in comparison to the handcrafted work of English cabinetmakers, the logo and symbol meant quality to many American buyers.

Advertisements in the *Furniture World* show that beginning in the mid-1890s, Stickley Brothers maintained a New York representative. By 1900, it also promoted a New York and London office, one for "domestic trade" and the other "export trade." As early as 1898, John George Stickley had made the New York office his frequent home. The Grand Rapids city directories indicate that in 1897, John George resided with Albert in his new mansion on Prospect Street. However, by 1898, the trade press noted that John George made his "headquarters in New York City."[48] Although John George was still listed as the vice president of Stickley Brothers, his move to New York became permanent in 1899, more than likely due to his impending marriage in New York City. The city directories listed John George as vice president of Stickley Brothers until at least 1900. However, during the next few years, his specific activities are unclear. The city directories list John George at one time or another representing Albert, Charles, and Leopold's enterprises, and at times all three simultaneously. It is clear that by 1902, he had joined forces with Leopold to form a company in Fayetteville, New York.[49]

Securely established and a well-known advocate of English design, Albert Stickley was in a firm position in 1900 as the shift and change began in American tastes toward more severe lines in style. Like Gustav, he began to make alterations in his designs for the new century. These were influenced by many of the same English and European sources that had inspired his older brother Gustav. However, Albert's frequent sojourns to England and Europe allowed him to build a repertoire of experience in all the various styles, which was reflected in his designs for the changing American market. The articulate Albert remained a practical furniture man throughout his career. However, his almost total dedication to his Arts & Crafts "Quaint" furniture brought the English style to America and won him national and international acclaim. He furnished as many of the American

46. *American Cabinetmaker and Upholsterer*, 7 July 1900, 18.

47. Christian Carron, "Grand Rapids Made," *Grand Rapids Furniture* (Traverse City, MI: Village Press, 1998), 69.

48. *American Cabinetmaker and Upholsterer*, 10 December 1898, 10.

49. When Leopold resigned from Gustav's company in September of 1902, it was on L. & J. G. Stickley stationery. The resignation letter is in the Stickley business records at Winterthur. Also see Cathers, *Furniture*, 76 for his notes on the changes of this period.

households, workplaces, clubs, and hotels in an Arts & Crafts style as Gustav Stickley or his other brothers did. In doing so, he became one of the movers and shakers in the new trend in American furniture design.

The exact date the Stickley Brothers introduced what might be considered an Arts & Crafts line to the American market more than likely occurred as early as 1899. There are hints in the various trade journals of Albert applying the lessons he had learned in Europe to the American trade. Already aware of the English preference for more severe designs without carving, he began in the summer of 1899 to introduce some English-designed pieces into the Grand Rapids market. In July, John Towse remarked, "There are any number of little details which give to the line of the Stickley Bros. Co, a distinctiveness and individuality this season. . . . the English novelties and the quaint little desk chairs will receive due attention. The finish on the company's goods is excellent."[50] By December, Towse again praised the new line to be introduced in 1900. He noted that "mahogany and oak are to be the principal woods. Some of the most exquisite effects are being produced in the company's marquetrie department and these will ornament the choicer pieces of the line. Stickley's goods are remarkably well finished and the high standing of excellence in this respect will be fully maintained. English velvets and tapestries will be largely used in upholstering."[51] In early 1900, after his trip to England to install E. E. Teal as the head of his London operation, Albert commented about the English preference for plain goods and noted that he had visited Paris just prior to the 1900 exposition and hoped that his new line of inlaid/marquetry furniture would be ready by the summer.[52]

By summer, the exposition had opened, and the American trade press as well as the furniture industry responded to the objects that were shown. By June, it seems that Stickley Brothers was already in production with some pieces based on what Albert had probably already seen. In addition, that June a report on the future of furniture based on the World's Fair appeared in the the *Grand Rapids Furniture Record*. The author reported on the winter Arts & Crafts exposition in Chicago and noted the "startling yet attractive designs" appearing in recent issues of the *Ladies' Home Journal*, which seemed to reflect what was going on in Europe. In conclusion, the author stated:

50. Towse, *Furniture World*, 13 July 1899, 49.

51. Towse, *Furniture World*, 23 December 1899, 33.

52. Towse, *Furniture World*, 15 March 1900, 25.

FROM THE NANCY SCHOOL
STICKLEY BROS. CO., GRAND RAPIDS

Two-tiered marquetry table from the Nancy School–inspired line of Stickley Brothers, illustrated in the *Grand Rapids Furniture Record*, June 1900.

> In connection with the foregoing, but more especially the florid Nancy idea referred to therein, the *Record* man found the other day in the Stickley Brothers art department, some specimens, made by them, based on the scheme and coloring of the original Nancy stuff. We give herein on other pages photographic reproductions of the pieces made here, in Grand Rapids, as evidence of the enterprise and advancement of the manufacturers of this Nancy of America. The pictures do not speak as plainly for themselves as if printed in col-

Mahogany and marquetry two-tiered tables by Louis Majorelle and Emile Gallé.

Mahogany breakfront carved with apple blossoms and boughs, 1900. From a dining room suite by Vincent Epeaux for the Exposition Universalle, Paris, and the winner of a silver medal.

53. "What of the Future," *Grand Rapids Furniture Record*, 1 June 1900, 26.

54. Ibid., 35.

55. Gabriel P. Weisberg, "Moulding Wood: Craftsmanship in Furniture," in *Art Nouveau: 1890–1914*, Paul Greenhalgh, ed. (New York: Harry N. Abrams, Inc., 2000), 172.

ors and which in the pieces are direct from nature. The decoration is marquetry. It is a reasonable prediction that they will come into favor, and rapidly, after they get a start." [53]

The pieces that appear in the pages of the *Grand Rapids Furniture Record* are far more elaborate than Gustav Stickley's simple Art Nouveau-style stands. The tables and stands by Stickley Brothers are more intricate, with elaborate marquetry on both the tops and sides. The tops are supported by turned posts and one table retains its claw feet.[54] Albert, like his brother Gustav, experimented with the new Art Nouveau styles.

Albert's visit to France only a few months before had informed him on the various schools of thought that would be represented at the World's Fair in Paris. The new French Art Nouveau designs exhibited at the fair fell into two groups: those that followed the approach of handcraftsmanship led by Siegfried Bing, who, in Paris, had coined the term *Art Nouveau*; and those who had followed Louis Marjorelle and Emile Gallé of Nancy, who emphasized the "mass production" of furniture. Gabriel Weisberg has pointed out that at Nancy "workmen produced several versions of the same piece of furniture. Suites of furniture were produced with almost assembly-line precision, a process that stood in stark contrast to the more traditional craftsman-like approach practiced by Bing in Paris."[55] Weisberg explained that many of the pieces emphasized wood inlay and that "expensive woods were frequently combined with elegant metal trimmings." This combination was ideal for Grand Rapids, where mass production was essential and virtually a manufacturing ethos.

Stickley Bros. Company

Grand Rapids, Mich

High=Grade and Medium

CHAIRS

Of all Kinds for all Purposes
Exclusive Designs
Original Drawings ✍ ✍ ✍

Reproductions and Modifications of the best
Antique, Colonial and Empire ✍ ✍ ✍ ✍ ✍ ✍ ✍

Wares for Export Trade, LONDON SALESROOM, 71 Paul Street
Wares for Domestic Trade, NEW YORK OFFICE, 33 Union Square

Stickley Brothers "Balmoral Settee," with decoration of inlaid birds and conventionalized trees, about 1902.

Opposite: Stickley Brothers oak settle, inlaid with stylized floral and fleur-de-lis motifs.

Albert Stickley was in a particularly good position to adapt quickly to the new ideas. Like Gustav, his flirtation with pure Art Nouveau would be brief, as he next turned to the British and Scottish for his inspirations. In the December issue of the *Grand Rapids Furniture Record* there also appear advertisements for chairs inspired by the English Arts & Crafts. These chairs are derivative of the work of English architects and designers such as A. H. Mackmurdo and C. F. A. Voysey. From the mid-1890s, the work of both Mackmurdo and Voysey, or copies of it, was frequently seen in England. Albert Stickley and his London-based company would have not only been aware of but also capable of executing such designs. These works also have the intricate inlay and British velvet tapestries of the English Arts & Crafts movement.

Writers from the trade press were often profuse in their praise of the inlaid work of the Stickley brothers. Such work was common in Britain and an essential part of much of the Nancy school. David Cathers has shown that much of Gustav Stickley's inlay work was contracted out to George H. Jones of New York City.[56] By contrast, Albert's inlay designer, T. A. Conti, was employed by the company. Conti was well respected for the quality of his inlay design work. He first appears in the Grand Rapids City Directory in 1897 and, by 1900, is listed as a designer for Stickley Brothers. He seems to have been specifically employed as a designer for inlay work, because E. Edmundson Dryden had

56. David Cathers, "Gustav Stickley, George H. Jones and the Making of Inlaid Craftsman Furniture," *Style 1900*, February 2000, 54-60.

Stickley Brothers rocker with tapered slats, model 736, about 1901.

been hired as the company designer in 1898 and remained in the position after Conti was hired. Conti continued to work for the company until 1904, when he began his own company with his sons and accepted free-lance work for others as well. During his employment with Stickley Brothers, he produced some of the best inlay work in Grand Rapids.

As early as August 1900, the Mission line had been introduced and advertised in the *Grand Rapids Furniture Record*. Advertisements from August on began to show variations on rectilinear or straight-line furniture designs with no ornamentation. The first pieces—simple suites, stools, and stands—were likely designed by Dryden. By February of 1901, Stickley Brothers had made further innovations in its straight-line furniture. In February, the *Record* praised the various Art Nouveau pieces and reported the addition of "a new wrinkle in leather bottoms and backs [of the Mission pieces] with a leather lacing used in upholstering the same, no tacks of any kind being used."[57]

In July of 1901, the *Grand Rapids Furniture Record* still touted Conti's skills but also high-lighted the Stickley Brothers new Mission line. In a survey of the Grand Rapids midsummer furni-ture exposition, they summarized the Stickley line by commenting on the company's success with standard historical styles, by pointing out:

> . . . In addition to the chairs and rockers, however, there is a fine line of den pieces, com-prising many exclusive designs and original drawings, with more than the usual number of new novelties in this line. Some very clever den tables of general utility, leather covered tables on the latest fad, the Mission order, also some rockers and chairs in the same style, among the newest pieces.
>
> It is of course known to the most prominent dealers but it should be a matter of local pride to know that there is undoubtedly no finer inlay work done in the world than that at Stickley Brothers Company. The finest artist in that special line is employed by this firm and the result of his skill and taste is apparent in his superb inlaid tables, chairs and rockers now on exhibit at the factory.[58]

At this point, it would seem that Albert and Gustav were moving in tandem with their experimen-tation and innovation. Some of their work was even similar in structure and form of design. However, they were not alone in their work with straight-line, rectilinear furniture designs. For example, in the same survey, the Michigan Chair Company was praised for its English-designed "straddle chair" and its "Mission chairs, magazine stands, [and] shaving glass cabinet."[59] Interestingly, the factories of the Michigan Chair Company and Stickley Brothers shared adjoining factory walls in Grand Rapids.

For the remainder of 1901 and through the first half of 1902, various advertisements demon-

57. "The Spring Exhibition Sale," *Grand Rapids Furniture Record*, 25 February 1901, 226.

58. "Mid-Summer Exhibition Sale," *Grand Rapids Furniture Record*, 1 July 1901, 42.

59. Ibid.

strate an evolution in the Stickley Brothers Arts & Crafts line. The various suites began to use more square posts instead of flat boards, and the overall line became more massive. However, it was not until the summer of 1902, with the hiring of David Robertson Smith as their designer, that Stickley Brothers began to take on a new and particularly innovative look. Smith would turn the company in an innovative design direction and lead it to national and international fame.

David Robertson Smith was born in Aberdeen, Scotland. After spending several years doing advertising work as a commercial artist, he began to design furniture for the Bath Cabinetmakers Company in England. Under the auspices of this company, in 1900, his work was exhibited in Paris where it was awarded " the highest award, including several gold and silver medals."[60] After leaving Bath, Smith moved to London and gained employment with Stickley Brothers at their London factory. Don Marek has conjectured that on his November 1901 trip to England, Albert asked Smith to come to America.[61] In early 1902, David Robertson Smith arrived in Grand Rapids. According to the Grand Rapids city directories, he replaced Stickley's designer, E. Edmundson Dryden, who went to work for Barber Brothers Chair Company. Smith was both a master commercial artist and

Stickley Brothers bedstead and bedside table from a bedroom suite, about 1903–1904.

60. "Factory Designers of Grand Rapids," *Furniture World*, 24 December 1908, 39.

61. Don Marek, "Introduction," *Quaint Furniture: Catalog No. 42*, reprint (Parchment, Michigan: Parchment Press, 1999), vi.

Cover of the *Grand Rapids Furniture Record* for June 1905, designed by David Robertson Smith.

Stickley Brothers Bewdley hexagonal inlaid oak Centre Table, about 1902. The inlay is a design of a stylized bud framed by leaves.

designer. He immediately set about redesigning the Stickley Brothers line with his introduction of what eventually would be called Quaint furniture. In commercial art, he redesigned and redefined the Stickley Brothers public image.

By the summer of 1902, Smith's commercial work promoting Stickley's new image began to appear in the various trade journals. Before the end of 1902, Stickley Brothers issued a new catalog filled with David Robertson Smith's designs for the company's Quaint furniture, including the Bewdley Suite. The catalog contains an extensive introduction explaining the furniture and its design philosophy. It was probably written by Smith because in September of 1902, he authored a similar article for the *Furniture Record* based almost word for word on this introduction.[62] Also in September, another report appeared with corresponding photographs of Albert's newly designed office filled with the new Quaint furniture, consisting of everything from settles to lighting fixtures and all designed by Smith.[63]

The introduction to the 1902 catalog is particularly informative. It explains the purpose of the catalog, defines the style, and indicates the source of its inspiration. The catalog's purpose was to show a limited number of pieces and tell "the 'whys' and 'wherefores' of our coming style."[64] The author points out that this new style was designed "to form a distinctive style of modern furniture and decoration." It notes that the attempt to design furniture for the modern man based on historical styles has failed "owing to the fact that those styles are not suited to present conditions and requirements."[65] It indicated that modern man was out of place in such furnishings. The new modern design "should be in keeping with the quiet dress of the period, neither profuse in rich ornamentation, nor yet blatant in the vigor of its plain simplicity. When a style is selected for the furnishing of a room, that style should be adhered to throughout the entire decoration."[66]

What may be most important for us is the emphasis on the formation of the style and the observation of the evolutionary process that Albert Stickley reiterated twenty-four years before his death. For example, in a discussion of the "New Century style," Smith explained that it:

> . . . is in process of formation, a modern style, which is to be characteristically its own, borrowing from the past only those features which are in accordance with present day requirements. Utility and simplicity form the guiding spirit of the new school, decorative lines being introduced to relieve the severity of the too many straight lines of the simple Mission furniture. The decoration will consist chiefly of marquetry of quaint, simple decorative lines, and purely conventional. Simple carving is also introduced, but will be kept entirely separate from the inlay work. Metal decorations, such as brass, copper and pewter, will also be judiciously used in the form of binding straps, hinge and escutcheon plates, etc."[67]

Smith advocated that the style was modern, that it drew upon the past but was constantly evolving and in a state of flux. In contrast to Gustav's work, subdued ornamentation was permitted—principally inlay, but also simple carving and metalwork. This new style would "most likely be called Quaint, or Quaint Decorative Furniture."

62. Compare David Robertson Smith, "Quaint Furniture," *Grand Rapids Furniture Record*, September 1902, 345-347.

63. "One Manufacturer's Fine Office," *Grand Rapids Furniture Record*, September 1902, 373-374.

64. *Stickley Brothers, Quaint Furniture* (Grand Rapids, MI: Stickley Brothers Furniture Company, 1902), 1.

65. Ibid.

66. Ibid., 2.

67. Ibid., 2f.

Detail of the carved owl from the Center Table.

Stickley Brothers Center Table with decoration of carved owls.

68. Ibid., 4.

The source of inspiration for the new style of furniture was also clearly stated. It was not to be found in Mission style, but in Scotland. The "ideals of William Morris and Burne-Jones, both Scots by blood, have been handed down and followed with an ever-widening influence, fostered and blended with the ideas of modern artists and bodies of artists, formed into societies such as the Guilded Crafts of Scotland and the Arts & Crafts of London."[68] This would not have been unusual since Smith was from Scotland and had worked in England before coming to Grand Rapids. Naturally, his tastes in design would reflect his training.

Several pieces that reflect the introductory description are pictured in the catalog. The cube settle and armchair in the Atholl suite have slatted backs and post legs bound to the arms with ornamented metal straps. Curves on the top rails and the slats that support the rails break the basic rectilinear scheme. The center slat and part of the top rail of the settle are decorated with inlay. The cushions are laced together and made of "nicely variegated leather." The overall effect is in sharp contrast to Gustav Stickley's work during the same time. It is the ornamentation that first strikes one as being so different from Gustav's simple, plain lines. Other pieces in the catalog have cutout slats, attenuated legs, and flat posts that are distinctively different from Gustav's orientation. Perhaps the greatest contrast can be found in the slightly ostentatious Bewdley suite, with carving and inlay that cover much of the surface of each piece.

Disregarding the Bewdley suite, there are several pieces that are aesthetically pleasing and that foreshadow much of what was to come in the Stickley Brothers line. For example, the Balmoral writing desk with its slanted top is nicely proportioned. The decoration of inlaid birds and trees that frame the gallery over the slant top highlight the front apron. The quartersawn white oak is well selected and gives harmony to the piece. The tapered or attenuated legs are a feature of the Stickley Brothers line, as are the Mackmurdo feet seen on the Dunross table. These characteristic details would become stylistic traits and remain even as the line evolved.

Stickley Brothers Bewdley Writing Desk, with dull brown copper and inlaid decoration, about 1902. This writing desk was part of a large suite of furniture that consisted of stools, a settee, a lounge couch, armchairs, bookcases, cellarette, cuspidor cases, and other complementary pieces.

The new designs by Smith marked a new direction for the Stickley Brothers' work. They were a blend of the work of both Conti and Smith. The catalog emphasizes how they avoided "incongruous styles": "To satisfy their desires to furnish their rooms artistically correct, the artist who designed the pieces employed an experienced cabinet maker, and they worked together, blending art with craft, with desired result."[69] The result was an effective interplay between workmanship, design, and decoration.

After the new furniture was introduced at the January 1903 exposition in Grand Rapids, Smith began to create an even more elaborate line. By the following summer, a new catalog was published, and it included a more comprehensive line of furniture for the library and den. The new line contained both English-influenced pieces and work that had a more traditional Mission look. Some objects included beautifully subdued inlay done by Conti, while other more massive pieces used through-tenon construction and keyed and tenon joinery. Again, the work in this catalog has a distinctively different feel when compared to the designs of Gustav Stickley. The tops of posts are often rounded rather than square or pyramidal. The characteristic Mackmurdo feet are frequently found on the various tables. Round cutouts appear as a motif all through a suite of chairs, magazine stands, desks, and bookcases. Although some pieces are lighter, others are massive in their construction. Large leather cushions with leather laces are a standard feature. The hardware has a chemically induced patina and is conventional in design. The overall effect of the work illustrates its English and Scottish heritage, easily recognizable to the knowledgeable critics.

The new line and David Robertson Smith's designs impressed the "furniture city." In December of 1903, the *Grand Rapids Furniture Record* announced the reopening of the lavish New Lakeside Club, which had been destroyed by fire in September of 1902. A major stained-glass window and one of the rooms was redone by Smith and Stickley Brothers. One author noted:

From the rear of the lobby rises the grand stair case, at the head of which are the steward's office and the clerk's desks. Behind the desks and opening into the office of the secretary of the club is a large semi-circular cathedral glass window, designed by D. Robertson Smith, of the Stickley Brothers' Company. The decorative idea expressed in this window is that of the spreading tail of a peacock and from the inner room the effect is extremely beautiful.[70]

69. Ibid., 2.

70. "Almost a Furniture Men's Club House," *Grand Rapids Furniture Record*, December 1903, 61.

Smith was also involved with the interior design of other parts of the building. He designed the English grill room, and it was furnished with Stickley Brothers Quaint furniture. Here the reviewer noted that Smith had 'made the entire furniture and finishings, including the copper chandeliers. This is one of the most novel and attractive features of the entire club house, and has been highly complimented and admired by every visitor to the club house."[71] Smith believed lighting was an important part of the environment. As he noted in his earlier article:

> The electric light fittings, which is one of the most important features to be considered in completing the furnishing of a room, offer great opportunities for good metal work. There is nothing more delicate than this illumination, and it lends itself to the broadest and most dainty forms. The conditions are nothing like what they were when we only had gas, and the great thing in designing is to let the metal work emphasize the delicacy and softness of the light.[72]

The use of electric light was a design element for Smith. He used it here and, as Marek has pointed out, he used it equally well in the design of Albert Stickley's office.[73] Marek has also suggested that it was Smith who was "most likely the impetus behind the formation of the Stickley Brothers Company copper shop." Smith seemed to be able to use all the means at his disposal to create an Arts & Crafts environment, which was basic to his design approach. He had carried out this theme of unity here in Stickley's office and in the club. However, within another year, Smith would lead Stickley Brothers to an even greater prize.

In 1904, the Louisiana Purchase Exhibition was held in St. Louis, Missouri. In December of 1903, the Grand Rapids Furniture Association met and decided to exhibit objects as a group and divide up the space allotted to them. Stickley Brothers obtained part of the space, and Smith designed the pieces for the exhibit. The results were even more successful than the work he had done for the Bath company in 1900. This time he won the Grand Prix for Albert and a gold medal for himself.[74] These pieces represent some of Smith's best work. The World's Fair exhibit by Stickley Brothers consisted of furniture for a den, library and a dining room suite. Most of the pieces included conventionalized copper-worked hinges, straps, and inlay by Conti. Working in both oak and mahogany, Stickley Brothers again created pieces quite unlike Gustav's work. The den suite included an inlaid drop-arm settle and a drop-front desk with leaded-glass doors. Smith's use of stained glass in his interiors was not limited to windows. In September of 1902, he commented on the importance of glass in the design of the interior and its furnishings. He wrote:

> Stained, or what is now known as leaded, glass is also taking a very strong hold in connection with our new Quaint style. In ages gone, stained glass was only used in Gothic windows, but now we have many uses for it, such as interior door panels, panels in sideboards and cabinets, and in some cases used as decorative wall friezes, illuminated from behind.

71. Ibid.

72. David Robertson Smith, "Quaint Furniture," *Grand Rapids Furniture Record*, September 1902, 347.

73. Marek, "Introduction," *Quaint Furniture: Catalog No. 42*, vi.

74. Ibid.

Above: Fumed-oak drop-front desk with leaded-glass doors from the award-winning Quaint Den Suite, exhibited by Stickley Brothers at the Varied Industries Building, The Louisiana Purchase Exposition, St. Louis, 1904. The furniture exhibited at St. Louis was published in the *Grand Rapids Furniture Record,* June 1904.

Opposite: A drop-arm settle from the Quaint Den Suite, the *Grand Rapids Furniture Record,* June 1904.

> An important feature of modern stained glass is the prominence given to outline. The lead, formerly looked upon as a necessary evil, has now become the most important feature. Where formerly it was the practice to exhibit a pictorial effect of color, the tendency is now to give fullest prominence to the leading decorative lines of lead, and then choosing and filling in the glasses to give the relief and the best effect of masses, and at the same time attaining due value to the general effect.[75]

75. Smith, "Quaint Furniture," 347.

Here in the desk, the leading echoes the conventionalized forms of the inlaid woods so delicately rendered by Conti, the master craftsman.

The unified dining room suite, consisting of a china cabinet, sideboard, and server, was also a success. All three had shoe feet and were crafted in fumed, quartersawn white oak. The copper strap hinges ended in a symbolic heart, reminiscent of Voysey themes and other conventionalized forms. As with the other forms in the exhibit, the copper work was created specifically for each piece. The eye is drawn to the center of each piece, where the inverted arch of chamfered boards is rounded off in typical Smith fashion. The overhanging tops are supported by small, functional corbels that enhance rather than detract from the proportions. Across the backsplash, each post also carries out the inverted arch at its top. The overall effect owes its heritage to the English/Scottish Arts & Crafts movement. If one compares the pieces from this dining room with Gustav Stickley pieces of the same period, the distance between them is clear. It is the distance between Europe and America.

Albert Stickley and David Robertson Smith brought England to America and impressed even the native Scots in the process.

Stickley Brothers' identification with the Scots gave a pleasant pause to J. Taylor of Glasgow, Scotland, in his review of the exhibition for the *Grand Rapids Furniture Record*. After condemning most of the exhibition as a "meager display," he praised the Stickley Brothers exhibit, especially for the unity of its display. He wrote, "I do not hesitate to say that this was one of the most artistic examples of a composite decorative scheme in the whole exposition."[76] He continued: "But in such rooms as those of Stickley Brothers Company you can trace the idea of the designer and follow out the unity of the scheme. And this is one of the points that makes the contemplation of examples of the new art so interesting and instructive."[77] He particularly singled out the use of cushions rather than springs and the lighting. In the dining room display he praised "the lighting from the pretty central electrolier and the supplementary lamps forming terminals to the pilasters all around the room supporting the china shelf."[78] The Scottish critic seemed to reiterate much of the philosophy behind the work of David Robertson Smith as published in his earlier articles on the new Quaint furniture and its purpose.

David Robertson Smith's success at the World's Fair made him a prominent figure among the Grand Rapids designers. Within a year, he began to accept freelance work, as had Conti in January of 1903. By the end of 1904, both Conti and Smith were listed in the city directories as living at the

76. J. Taylor, "American Furniture at the World's Fair," *Grand Rapids Furniture Record*, July 1904, 256.

77. Ibid., 258.

78. Ibid.

same residence and as freelance designers. It was not uncommon for Stickley Brothers employees to freelance. For example, Don Marek has traced the development of the Stickley Brothers copper shop, which employed multiple designers and craftsmen who eventually opened their own shops.[79] The shop opened sometime in 1904 "because of the need for specialized copper and brass furniture hardware" in the Stickley factory. The shop had offered a variety of items, including the lamp fixtures designed by Smith. However, as Marek notes, "despite the success of the shops, their work under the Stickley Brothers Company umbrella ended by 1907, and the workmen formed independent shops."[80] Marek pointed out that Stickley Brothers continued to market the copper shop goods until 1912, but the goods were purchased directly from the independent makers and designers.

79. Don Marek, *Grand Rapids Art Metalwork: 1902–1928* (Grand Rapids, MI: Heartwood, 1999), 57-61.

80. Ibid., 59.

Opposite: Oak china cabinet with hand-wrought copper hardware and decorative elements, from the award-winning Quaint Dining Room Suite, exhibited by Stickley Brothers at the Louisiana Purchase Exposition, St. Louis, 1904.

Below: Oak sideboard with hand-wrought copper hardware from the Quaint Dining Room Suite, exhibited by Stickley Brothers at the Louisiana Purchase Exposition, St. Louis, 1904.

101

81. John Towse,
"Opening of the
Sales," *Furniture
World*, 22 June 1905,
37.

Almost immediately, Stickley Brothers placed advertisements in the trade journals announcing their awards at St. Louis. In the summer of 1904, Albert Stickley was elected president of the Grand Rapids Furniture Association and then reelected the following year.[81] He was recognized as one of the foremost leaders in the furniture industry. Other successes quickly followed. In November, the company received a commission to create the furniture for the famous new El Tovar Hotel, at Grand Canyon, Arizona, including a specially designed large sideboard and screen for the dining room.

> The sideboard is ten feet eight inches long, six feet four inches high and two feet two inches deep, with solid copper trimmings. The screen is ten feet ten inches long, seven feet two inches high. The panels are of leather, showing the coat-of-arms or crest of Pedro del Tovar, after whom the hotel is named. On the corner posts of the screen are six large electric lamps. The sideboard and screen are of fumed oak.[82]

82. "Magnificent
Sideboard and
Screen," *Grand
Rapids Furniture
Record*, November
1904, 770.

Existing photographs show that Stickley Brothers chairs and tables from the regular catalog appeared throughout the rest of the building and that the company had outfitted the vast majority of the prestigious hotel with its furniture. However, the most striking piece was the massive sideboard and its accompanying screen, which had a lamp atop each of the six tall Mackmurdo/Voysey–style posts. Again, there is dramatic contrast between the rustic simplicity of Gustav's specialized pieces and this sideboard. The sideboard is backed by beveled panels instead of chamfered boards. The two large, covered, recessed areas on each side become equal but separate pieces and are linked by a subordinate center section that is dominated by the screen behind it. The design lacks the strap hinges seen in Gustav Stickley's pieces or in the World's Fair suite, opting for simple pulls instead. Designed as it was for a commercial hotel, the piece works quite well.

Opposite:
The Rendezvous at the
Hotel El Tovar, Grand
Canyon National Park,
Arizona, furnished by
Stickley Brothers.

Above:
The main dining room at
the Hotel El Tovar, with the
Stickley Brothers sideboard
on the left and two model
8610 buffets on the right.

Right:
Private dining room at the
Hotel El Tovar, Grand
Canyon National Park,
Arizona, about 1904–1905.
The furniture in the room
includes a model 8610 buf-
fet, an unidentified dining
table and model 412^{1}/$_{2}$ din-
ing chairs.

Stickley Bros. Co., Grand Rapids, Mich.

By the end of 1904, Stickley Brothers were primarily producing furniture for the den, library, and dining room for the home; the club and café; and other commercial uses. Emphasis on these lines seems to have continued throughout 1905. However, in August of 1905, a change was indicated in an advertisement in the *Grand Rapids Furniture Record*. It announced that a "supplementary catalogue [is] now ready" and included a line drawing, probably from a catalog, like the illustrations that appeared in several issues of the *Grand Rapids Furniture Record* during the second half of 1904.[83] The advertisement also promised new designs for the fall. By December of 1905, Stickley Brothers introduced new extensions to the line with designs for the "Library, Sitting Room, Bed Room, Office, Club and Café" as well as "Russian Hand Beaten Copper." [84] From this point onward, the company devoted its major energy toward the domestic marketing of their Quaint furniture line that was suited "for the entire house." The December advertisement also offered a "booklet with suggestions for arrangement and interior decoration, together with catalogue, mailed on request." The new catalog offered in December departed from traditional line drawings, offering half-tone photographs of the items.

After 1906, Stickley Brothers seemed to be totally dedicated to its Arts & Crafts line for the domestic market. In July, for the summer furniture exposition, they opened a showroom with a functional café outfitted with Stickley Brothers furniture.[85] The last advertisements for "fancy rocker" lines appeared in 1903, and apparently the line did not change again until 1909 with the introduction of the Tudor line.

It is unclear when the firm ceased its London operations, but Marek has suggested 1904 as a terminal date because that is the last reference he found to Albert sending products to England.[86]

83. Advertisement for
Stickley Brothers,
*Grand Rapids
Furniture Record*, 1
November 1905,
356.

84. Advertisement for
Stickley Brothers,
*Grand Rapids
Furniture Record*,
December 1905, 14.

85. "What the Present
Season Has Brought
Forth," *Grand Rapids
Furniture Record*,
July, 1906, 253. See
also photograph of
the café in the
*Grand Rapids
Furniture Record*,
August 1906, 371.

86. Marek,
"Introduction,"
*Quaint Furniture:
Catalog No. 42*, vi.

Marek is probably correct in his assumption, because in October of 1904 an article by Albert Stickley appeared in the *Grand Rapids Furniture Record* that complained bitterly of the comparison between English handmade and American machine-made furniture. He indicated that the comparison was unfair because of the cost difference between the goods. He noted that "no machine can turn out as nicely finished an article as can the human hand." However, he indicated that products created by hand are too expensive for the middle class. He concluded with an interesting note that "it does not pay the American manufacturers to work very hard for English patronage because it is so limited.[87]

In the years between 1906 and 1910, the Stickley Brothers Quaint Arts & Crafts line reached its maturity. After its initial expansion into an extended line, the firm slowly discontinued a number of Smith's more radical designs. They were replaced by more mainstream rectilinear furniture. The company now stabilized its focus on its more conservative and middle-range objects. However, its Quaint line remained in production throughout most of the teens, as did similar lines manufactured by other firms.

87. Albert Stickley, "English Hand-Made and American Machine-Made Furniture," *Grand Rapids Furniture Record*, October 1904, 641.

Below: Stickley Brothers oak settle with canted sides, model 3863, about 1905.

Above:
Stickley Brothers oak Library Table with copper hardware, model 2680, about 1906.

Below:
Stickley Brothers settee, model 3861, introduced in 1904 as part of a library suite.

By 1906, almost every furniture company had a Mission line, and the competition was keen. Stickley Brothers remained competitive throughout the period by offering other incentives, beyond their copper products, to their line. Items such as waxes, finishes, and goatskin pillows were also produced for the market.

Other company designers introduced new designs and settings that adapted Albert's English Arts & Crafts line to changing trends. Between 1908 and 1911, Arthur E. Teal was the company designer. During his tenure, he executed several interior designs that appeared in the *Grand Rapids Furniture Record*. The images pictured dining rooms, reception rooms and libraries, appropriately filled with Stickley Brothers furnishings. These settings represented Albert's ideal of the American home. However, Teal's drawings held more of an English Arts & Crafts character that sharply contrasted with Gustav's interiors. Teal's color rendering of a dining room, done with a strong red overtone, is completely equipped with Stickley Brothers furniture, all with softly rounded shapes in keeping with Albert's and even Smith's design concepts for Arts & Crafts. Although Stickley Brothers had made commercial hall seats similar to those by the hearth in this drawing, these are tucked away from the rest of the room as built-in inglenooks. A Stickley Brothers lamp is suspended over the table from the beamed ceiling, and the company's copper is amply displayed throughout the room on plate rails. The room seems particularly dark, and the eye is drawn to the glow of the hearth. Again, the room has a different feel from Gustav Stickley's earlier well-lighted interiors with stained glass windows and architectural built-ins based on German rather than English models. For example, the alternating inset spaces on the walls of Gustav's 1905 living room are taken directly from his observations of the German exhibit at the World's Fair. The wall treatments for Gustav's interiors are open, with less to disrupt the eye as it moves about the room. Objects are placed specifically as part of the architectural unity. For example, vases are often placed into recesses after the German manner adapted from the World's Fair exhibit. However, the furniture in Gustav's interior, even with its sweeping horizontal arches, has harder edges than Albert's. In the final analysis, Albert's work is different from Gustav's in its tone and design even though it may feed from some of the same European sources. In any case, neither brother produced direct copies of European pieces, but amalgams from multiple sources, put together in different ways.

In 1909, Albert was still extolling the "merits of Arts & Crafts." In an article by the same name, he warned that Arts & Crafts style could be "subject to deterioration and injury, through lack of appreciation, skill, designer and maker, as any other style or type."[88] He noted that "[m]any people confuse the Mission with the Arts & Crafts." After a discussion of the movement's development, he indicated that in Europe today "there is no question but what the most popular style in architecture, carpetings, fabrics, furniture, pottery, jewelry, etc., is the Arts & Crafts, built on popular structural lines." He praised British design through the words of Reginald Bloomfield: "Three great qualities stamped the English tradition in furniture so long as it was a living force—steadfastness of purpose, reserve in design, and thorough workmanship." Structure was to be emphasized and "exemplified in two ways: first, the greatest possible amount of structural strength and dignity should be obtained with the smallest possible amount of wood; and next, the wood must be handled expertly as wood, and not made to simulate the properties of any other material."[89]

88. Albert Stickley, "Merits of Arts & Crafts," *Furniture*, April 1909, 30.

89. Ibid.

A dining room in
Quaint Arts and
Crafts designed
by Arthur E. Teal
for Stickley
Brothers in 1908.
Teal's monogram
appears in the
lower right cor-
ner.

Albert concluded by simply advocating "reasonableness in quiet design and good construction."

However, by 1909, the Stickley Brothers Arts & Crafts line was almost completely devoid of Smith's original designs, and only a few chairs remained that bore any resemblance to the older forms. By now, most had been converted into simple rectilinear forms that lacked the rounded edges of the earlier forms and carefully worked hardware of the old copper shop. Some of Smith's elements, such as the proverbial Mackmurdo feet, were retained, but much of the softness was gone. Although Stickley Brothers claimed in its advertisements in 1909 that the firm's work was difficult to imitate, most companies in Grand Rapids, as well as elsewhere, came very close. Their line, even with the earlier forms, was identified with Mission. Although many of the basic older forms continued to be produced for years, Albert was more than willing to change and alter his style in order to compete.

In 1909, the company introduced a Tudor line of Quaint furniture. Tudor was based on Stickley's basic Arts & Crafts line, but with the addition of turned legs. The advertisements freely admitted that the line was "the result of the adaptation of certain harmonious and characteristic lines and feature of some of the most meritorious furniture made in England during the reigns of the English Tudors." [90] They discontinued their traditional cushions in favor of ones known as

90. Stickley Brothers
advertisement,
*Grand Rapids
Furniture Record,*
September 1909,
438.

English double spring cushions. In the same month, they also introduced their English Upholstered Furniture line, which consisted of fifty new models of chairs and couches.

After 1910, many manufacturers returned to various historical styles as the demand for lighter furniture won favor with the public. A whole gamut of historical styles appeared, ranging from William and Mary to Jacobean and the proverbial colonial styles. However, some companies, such as Stickley Brothers and Gustav Stickley, introduced their own blending of the new styles.

By the middle of the decade, Stickley Brothers offered the same variety of historical styles as other manufacturers. Nevertheless, in December of 1913, it introduced a new Manor style that was to be a blend of both Austrian and English sources. The *Grand Rapids Furniture Record* formally announced the introduction of their new line, one produced to meet the public demand for furniture that was "smaller and lighter" than Quaint Mission. The new line was described as:

> . . . the best England has produced in modern style, and embodies the original Austrian interpretation and adaptation which brought this style into such general favor on the continent. It represents in Europe the last word in their modern design, just as Quaint Mission does the American modern style.[91]

Reception room in Quaint Arts and Crafts designed by Arthur E. Teal for Stickley Brothers in 1908. Teal's monogram appears in the lower left corner.

91. Stickley Brothers advertisement, *Grand Rapids Furniture Record*, December 1914, 1106.

Dining room designed by David Robinson Smith for Stickley Brothers, the *Grand Rapids Furniture Record*, September 1905.

In 1914, Stickley Brothers issued a new catalog for the emerging set of tastes that had developed since the beginning of the second decade. The catalog showed a variety of finishes and several styles. The inlaid items were replaced by painted designs and enamel finishes. In order to adapt to the many changes in the furniture trade, the Arts & Crafts lines became lighter. The following note appeared with one of their advertisements for their patterns of "quaint Manor and Elizabethan on the exhibition floor":

> The Stickley Bros. organization has never been deaf to the best interests of the Dealer. When the mission influence was at its height, Stickley Bros. dignified the motif in Quaint Mission Pattern—a pure American style, the success of which is reflected in its unwaning leadership in scores of retail institutions. The English influence, no less insistent than the Mission, has been interpreted in the latest Stickley Bros. creation—Quaint Elizabethan Furniture.[92]

92. Stickley Brothers advertisement, *Grand Rapids Furniture Record*, November 1914, 6.

Although he listened to the public and adapted to the ever-changing times, Albert Stickley still praised things English and European. Although he no longer maintained an English factory he continued to travel to Europe, making trips in 1910 and 1913.

**Dining room by
Stickley Brothers,
the *Grand Rapids
Furniture Record*,
March 1906.**

As we have seen, by 1914 Gustav Stickley was feeling the pressure of change, and the same was true of Albert Stickley. However, before Gustav introduced his Chromewald line as a reaction to the changes, Albert was operating on several different fronts in order to capture the market. Don Marek has pointed out:

> This must have been a difficult time for Albert Stickley, as he tried to move his company in a new direction. He seems to have hedged his bets somewhat by moving in opposite directions—introducing Jacobean and Elizabethan lines and a line based on Austrian Modern at the same time. If that was not confusing enough, he sometimes combined the styles in the same piece of furniture, resulting in some truly aberrant designs.[93]

The new designs were not failures, and Albert continued to have a profitable business. In fact, when he introduced the new lines in January of 1914, he expanded by opening fully stocked warehouses on both coasts so that dealers could obtain goods on short notice.[94] The progressive thinking and marketing of his furniture continued. Marek points out that Albert continued to adapt ideas from his trips. He notes: "By 1917, he had traveled to Japan to recruit experienced hand-decorators to

93. Marek,
"Introduction,"
*Quaint Furniture:
Catalog No. 42*, vii.

94. Stickley Brothers
advertisement,
*Grand Rapids
Furniture Record*,
January 1914, 19.

95. Marek, "Introduction," *Quaint Furniture: Catalog No. 42*, viii.

work for him in Grand Rapids. Through the 1920s the company sold a great deal of hand-painted decoration." [95] Albert would remain involved not only in his own business but as part of the fledgling Associate Cabinet Makers formed by Gustav, Leopold, and John George after Gustav's bankruptcy in 1916. For a short period, the brothers, with the exception of Charles, would be together again. Albert's advertisements in 1917 in the *Grand Rapids Furniture Record* promoted Gustav's Chromewald finish on a regular basis. One advertisement even advertised his gift shop, where customers could purchase just about anything from lamps to aquariums.

Such innovations and adaptations continued until Albert's retirement in the mid-1920s. In 1924, his first wife, Jane Worden, died and soon afterward he married Emlyn Lewis. The couple retired to Gorgeic County in the upper peninsula of Michigan, where Albert built an elaborate lodge and entertained frequently. He lived there until his death, a few years later in 1928. The company continued under the name of Stickley Brothers in one form or another until 1947, but it would no longer be run by a family member.

Both Gustav and Albert Stickley were the most innovative of the Stickley brothers in the development of their style and forms. They worked on a national and even international basis. They traveled and understood the world of their craft from their journeys. They read and fully understood the principles but came from different perspectives on the style they approached—Arts & Crafts. At times, they seemed to work in tandem, both using the same sources. Still, for each brother the results were different. Their earliest forms set trends throughout the furniture industry.

It remained for Leopold Stickley to industrialize the Arts & Crafts form on an even wider scale. Leopold and John George would become a commercial team that milked the best out of the form and served as models for others to follow. Charles, too, would follow, showing his own brief independence in style and design. However, these are subjects for another chapter.

■ ■
**Stickley Brothers
settee in the
Elizabethan
style, about
1914.**

Charles, Leopold and John George's Contributions

Charles, Leopold, and John George were slower to make changes and more cautious than Gustav and Albert. Charles never left home, remaining in Binghamton throughout his life. His only journeys appear to have been regional and always linked with his and Schuyler Brandt's retail store or chair factory. Although clearly aware of the changes in tastes and fashion, Charles only had a brief period of innovation in the Arts & Crafts movement.

At the turn of the century, Leopold quickly joined forces with John George to form the L. & J. G. Stickley Furniture Company. This company, through its adaptability and shrewd business practices, may have been more influential than either Gustav or Albert in placing Arts & Crafts furniture in American homes. Because of such practices, even after John George's death, Leopold's company would survive and prosper.

CHARLES STICKLEY: THE BROTHER WHO STAYED BEHIND

The Stickley-Brandt Furniture Company (the retail store) and the Stickley & Brandt Chair Company (the factory)

Design for a living room by L. & J. G. Stickley originally published in the 1906 Handcraft catalog, the *Grand Rapids Furniture Record*, February 1908.

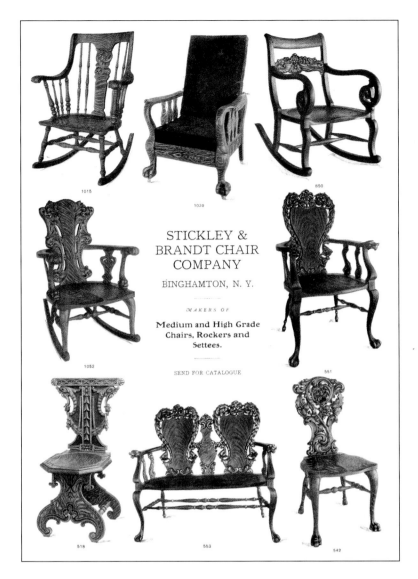

Stickley & Brandt advertisement picturing their ornate, traditionally designed chairs and rockers, the *Grand Rapids Furniture Record*, March 1904.

STICKLEY &
BRANDT CHAIR
COMPANY

BINGHAMTON, N. Y.

MAKERS OF

Medium and High Grade
Chairs, Rockers and
Settees.

SEND FOR CATALOGUE

1. The incorporation, with a capital stock of $30,000, was granted on December 30, 1891. Schuyler C. Brandt was president and Charles Stickley was manager. The Stickley-Brandt Furniture Company was incorporated on December 22, 1896, with Schuyler Brandt as president and Charles Stickley as vice president. The company finally folded in 1928.

2. John Towse, "Correspondence," *Furniture World,* 23 January 1899, 8

3. "The Stickley & Brandt Chair Co.," *American Cabinet Maker and Upholsterer,* 13 May 1899, 29.

were well-established and thriving enterprises in Binghamton, New York, by 1900.[1] Both companies were well known and respected throughout the Northeast and Midwest. Towse reported that 1899 was their best year in the furniture business,[2] and another article claimed, "Its goods are thoroughly known from Maine to California and bear an enviable reputation."[3] Schuyler C. Brandt was er of the factory.

After producing approximately 45,000 chairs in 1899, Charles and Schuyler decided to expand the chair company's facilities in 1900. They bought the Binghamton Wagon Company Building, which allowed them to double their output. They increased their number of workers from 150 to 200 with the expansion. The new facility was one of the best in the state. After the expansion they were well prepared and approached the new century with a sense of optimism.

By 1901, they were exhibiting yearly, both in Grand Rapids and at the New York furniture trade exposition. Their line was described by Towse as a "strictly high grade line of fancy chairs and rockers, including *L'Art Nouveau* innovations."[4] However, at this point, nothing produced by

Stickley and Brandt was similar in style or quality to the Arts & Crafts work being created by the other brothers in Grand Rapids and Syracuse. The only line that even slightly resembled Arts & Crafts was their "summer" furniture, which consisted of one lightweight suite with some cutouts in the legs and back slats. The rest of the line primarily consisted of "fancy," or elaborately carved, rockers and chairs. There were other pieces in traditional historical styles, but nothing that seemed unusual or avant-garde in any way.

In 1903, Schuyler left Binghamton for health reasons and began to represent the company in the "western territory."[5] This consisted of the area west of Buffalo, New York. He settled in Chicago and began exhibiting at the annual show in the Windy City. Until his death in 1913, Schuyler lived in Chicago but continued to hold the title of president of both companies in Binghamton. John George, who was living in New York City at the time, represented the area to the east. He continued to represent this area after he became the vice president of L. & J. G. Stickley. This arrangement only lasted about a year before I. H. Mannes took over the territory. At this point, the relationship between all of the brothers, even on a competitive basis, seems to have been amicable. For example, in the papers of Gustav Stickley during the Simonds years and later, there are frequent references to Gustav having sold items to Charles. There is an entry from May 1902 in the Gustav Stickley sales ledgers at Winterthur that lists the sale of six separate chairs to the Stickley & Brandt Furniture Company. In another instance, one document appears to be a record of loan of money from Gustav to Charles.[6] In later years, Gustav Stickley's hardware appeared on Charles's furniture lines, indicating an active trade between these two companies. There are also records of similar transactions and loans between Leopold and Gustav during this time. Such dealings seem to indicate a good business and possibly personal relationship among the brothers. As noted earlier, even when Gustav Stickley denounced his competition in his catalogs and named his brothers, it was a retail store, Kaufmann Brothers, that he attacked in court, not the furniture makers.

In 1904 and 1905, the Stickley & Brandt Chair Company staged an aggressive marketing campaign and issued a new catalog and line of some "75 to 85 new pieces." The 1905 advertisements pictured quartersawn oak Arts & Crafts–style chairs and rockers with cutouts, carved inlays, and lightweight designs, and sporting cane seats for the summer trade. Some of these characteristics an important role in Charles Stickley's later Arts & Crafts line. However, most of the chairs stayed within the more conservative fashions of the day. In many cases, the chairs were traditionally designed, excessively ornate, and only adequately constructed. Such work was very different from the principles articulated by Gustav, Albert, or even Leopold and John George in the middle of the first decade of the twentieth century. The advertisements and catalogs featured some pieces with turned legs and curved-and-scalloped, lightweight, pressed backs that appear to have been made from cheaper-grade goods.

From 1905 until the summer of 1909, the Stickley & Brandt Chair Company continued to prosper, but its designs remained conservatively fashionable and static. In 1906, the *Furniture World* summed up the line as follows: "Stickley & Brandt goods are not all of one grade. You may select some that are considered cheap, you may buy medium and fine, but I suppose the best appellation

4. "Stickley & Brandt Fire," *Furniture World*, 4 April 1895, 39; "Notes," Furniture World, 1 April 1897, 27; and "The Exchange Mirror," *Furniture World*, 24 January 1901, 27.

5. "Eastern Notes," *Furniture World*, 22 October 1903, 39. Schuyler's departure is confirmed by the city directories.

6. Letter from Charles Stickley to Gustav Stickley, 12 February 1902, Winterthur Library, Joseph Downs Collection, 76x101.2356. The letter discusses a loan made in 1893 from Gustav for $3106. Gustav Stickley hardware also appears frequently on Charles's Mission line, and they were involved in trying to set up the Chair Trust as were all the brothers during the late 1890s.

7. John Towse, "On the Road," *Furniture World*, 14 June 1906, 15.

8. John Towse, "On the Road," *Furniture World*, 24 December 1908, 13.

for the whole is 'medium.'" [7] It would seem that this line would hold little interest for the Arts & Crafts enthusiast. However, in December of 1908, a cryptic note appeared in the *Furniture World*. On a recent visit, the publication's correspondent was surprised that Charles Stickley was silent about his new line and noted, "I believe Stickley has something up his sleeve and at the proper time it will be sprung." [8]

Charles's surprise, the issue of his first full Arts & Crafts line, hit the markets in January of 1909. It seems to have been an immediate success. The *Furniture World* noted:

> The entire Stickley family is now engaged in the manufacture of mission and Arts & Crafts furniture. People in the trade have wondered why Charles Stickley didn't get into the game and make it unanimous. He had thought about it, all right, and last fall he finally got busy. The Stickley & Brandt Chair Co. came out in January with fifty pieces, individual chairs, rockers, settees, library tables and settles, and the same in suits. . . . The company is to have a larger line of chairs, rockers and settles and in addition ladies' desks, extension tables, side boards, china cabinets, side tables, stools, tabourettes, waste paper baskets and umbrella racks. The company will continue the regular line of chairs and rockers but will drop the cheap end of it. . . . A catalogue will be issued August 1. [9]

9. John Towse, "On the Road," *Furniture World*, 17 June 1909, 19.

In the months that followed, both the new Mission line called "Modern Craft" and a new "Flanders" line appeared to be selling well. By December, the company was known as a maker of Mission furniture. According to Towse, the new line exhibited in Grand Rapids was "second to none." He added that the "mission styles, beautifully catalogued, and differentiated by the leather tag of the Modern Craft shop, were designed and made under the direction of Charles Stickley. . . . The new furniture will be shown in Early English and fumed finishes. The company has perfected the fuming process, and its fumed oak cannot fade nor deteriorate." [10] It was not long before the line began to appear in homes and businesses throughout the country, from New York to the Deep South. One hotel in Georgia even outfitted its entire lobby with the distinct Charles Stickley chairs and rockers.

10. John Towse, "On the Road," *Furniture World*, 16 December 1909, 11.

11. John Towse, "On the Road," *Furniture World*, 8 June 1911, 17.

12. The signature was reproduced from the original by the Dill & Collins Company, paper manufacturers of Philadelphia and New York. It contains eight pages illustrating eleven pieces of furniture. The original catalog was designed, engraved, and printed by James Bayne Company, Grand Rapids, Michigan, on paper made by Dill & Collins.

By 1911, Charles devoted the entire line, about 175 pieces, to Mission and was phasing out the fancy rocker line. Towse indicated the line included "settees, rockers, ladies' desks, dining room, den, living room, library and bedroom furniture, and these novelties: Children's chairs and rockers, costumers, waste paper baskets, umbrella stands, plant and jardiniere stands, smokers' stands, and breakfast tables." [11] According to the *Furniture World*, Charles planned to introduce more Mission pieces for the fall and had issued a new catalog.

A signature of this catalog, reproduced by the Dill & Collins Company, is in the collections of the Henry Francis DuPont Winterthur Museum Library. [12] Portions of the foreword and images from the catalog were included in the *Furniture World*. Towse quoted the following from the foreword:

At no other time in the history of modern furniture production have the straight lines, the structural beauty and the supreme comfort of mission styles been so favored in American home decorations as at the present period. As produced by the Stickley & Brandt Chair Co. they have gained a widespread popularity. True to their motif, they have retained simplicity while developing soundness of structure, and their inherent beauty is made to depend mainly upon pure structural lines, whose first consideration is comfort and utility. Sound and lasting materials are employed. The well-cured wood is protected by a soft and artistic finish, which does not hide its natural beauty. Leathers are heavy and durable, and the pigments used in their coloring produce a subtle harmony with the simple beauty of the furniture in whose building they form a part. In preparing the models of this mission furniture, its designer has carefully studied and interpreted the trend of American ideas in housefurnishing. The return from the ornate to the simple and the growing desire for naturalness have found true expression in his designs.[13]

Interior of the Hotel Lanier in Macon, Georgia, furnished with chairs by Stickley & Brandt.

13. John Towse, "On the Road," *Furniture World*, 4 January 1912, 15.

The Modern Craft line and the catalog introduction cited in the *Furniture World* echo the introduction of a 1910 L. & J. G. Stickley catalog. They both place an emphasis on being functional and "scientifically" modern. In 1995, Donald Davidoff identified that this emphasis on functional, scientific, modern design separated the work of L. & J. G. Stickley from that of the Prairie school and

Stickley & Brandt double-door book-case with Gustav Stickley hardware, similar in design to Gustav Stickley's model 504 bookcase.

their derivations on Gustav Stickley's forms.[14] Charles now had over 200 pieces in his line and planned to increase it.

The catalog illustrations that appeared in the pages of the *Furniture World* seem to be either direct or close imitations of the work of Gustav Stickley or that of L. & J. G. Stickley. There is an almost exact imitation of Gustav Stickley's model 720 desk. The copy seems to be identical, down to the Gustav Stickley oval metal pulls on the drawers. These examples are reinforced by the number of items that have appeared in the marketplace that are reproductions of Gustav Stickley's other pieces. For example, Charles duplicated the popular Gustav Stickley model 715 and model 716 one-and-two door bookcases, which frequently appear with Gustav Stickley hardware. When Gustav Stickley's hardware is used on such pieces, they seem to become a direct imitation. Since Gustav had sold his hardware, it would not have been unusual for Charles to have used it on his copies of his older brother's work.

Many of Gustav's familiar techniques are also used on the bookcase. The doors show mullioned panes with stationary shelves along the line of the mullions. These shelves are all fully inset into the sides of the bookcase, and the top and lower shelves have tenons that go fully through the sides and are carefully softened, similar to the Craftsman model. The top and bottom boards are also fully pinned from the front of the sides. Wood selection for the doors and sides is also generally excellent and shows only the best of the quartersawn oak.

It is only when one looks closely that some of the shortcuts taken by Charles are visible. For example, the shelves are usually thinner, and the backs are often made of poplar. The backs are often chamfered or made of tongue-and-groove boards that lack the care and techniques used in Gustav Stickley originals. While many of the construction methods may be solid, they seem to lack the detail of the original model, making them of good, but not excellent, workmanship.

Charles also imitated the work created by his younger brothers Leopold and John George. The items are illustrated in the catalog as line drawings after the manner of L. & J. G. Stickley. The familiar L. & J. G. Stickley version of the trestle table is depicted but with larger, keyed tenons. A version of L. & J. G. Stickley's model 281 settle is copied as well. Other companies also copied this settle. For example, the J. M. Young and Sons Furniture Company of Camden, New York, made a very close copy of the model 281. By contrast, the drawing of the Charles Stickley model 1591 in the Winterthur copy of the catalog does not demonstrate the close affinity of this settle to the L. & J. G. Stickley original. Those that have shown up in the marketplace, however, are very close copies of the L. & J. G. Stickley original, with massive posts and excellent wood choices. They even have the same number of slats on the sides and in the back, making them almost identical copies. Given the speedy introduction of this line and the closeness of some of the imitations, there is reason to suspect that the work was being done with the help of both Leopold and John George. The Stickley brothers at this time were closely bound by family ties. It would be reasonable to speculate that all of the brothers in Syracuse worked closely with Charles and perhaps aided him with his new line of furniture.

However, the truly distinctive work of Charles Stickley does not appear in the pages of the *Furniture World* or the existing catalog signature. Perhaps Charles's strongest independent designs are the chairs and settles with the massive two-inch-by-four-inch front legs. There are a number of

14. See Donald A. Davidoff, "Innovations and Derivations: The Contribution of L. & J. G. Stickley to the Arts & Crafts Movement," *Innovation and Derivation: The Contribution of L. & J. G. Stickley to the Arts & Crafts Movement* (Morris Plains, NJ: The Craftsman Farms Foundation, 1995), 33-36 for an excellent analysis and *The Work of L. & J. G. Stickley* (Fayetteville, NY: L. & J. G. Stickley Company, nd), 2-5, for the primary source material.

■ ■

Left: Stickley & Brandt even arm settle based on L. & J. G. Stickley's model 281.

Below: L. & J. G. Stickley even arm settle, model 281.

variations on this design, with cutouts that seem to hark back to his earlier Art Nouveau chairs. The basic models have plain slatted backs and large arms with long through-tenons that are extensions of the large front legs. The legs are so well veneered that they appear quartersawn on all four sides, an impossibility.[15]

The most commonly seen three-piece group—a rocker, an armchair, and a settle—is innovative Charles Stickley at his best. These pieces were created early in his career as an Arts & Crafts designer and are identified by the small yellow decal/label of Stickley & Brandt rather than the branded signature that seems to appear on the later work.[16] Bruce Johnson speculates that the decal dates between 1909 and 1913 or until just after the death of Schuyler Brandt.[17] Although these chairs are certainly well built, they still maintain the false through-tenons that were so common among a number of other quality makers. While disturbing, a false through-tenon does not affect the quality of the joint in this case because it is a plug, and the joint is a mortise-and-tenon joint that

Chair with cutouts designed by Charles Stickley for Stickley & Brandt Chair Co., about 1910.

15. When any wood is cut, two sides must be plain sawn and the other two quartersawn. This means that the quartersawn wood would show the medullar rays of the wood to their best effect. The more the quartersawn side is shown, the more expensive the wood will be because of the enormous waste in the cutting process.

16. A circular blue-and-white paper label appears on the earlier pre-Mission pieces.

17. Bruce Johnson, *The Official Price Guide to Arts & Crafts*, 2nd ed. (New York: House of Collectibles, 1992), 105.

has been effectively pinned. However, the same cannot be said of all of Charles Stickley's work. Many of the pieces bearing the branded signature labels often have drawbacks such as weaker construction through doweled joints, inadequate proportions in design, and poorer wood choices.

As several individuals have suggested, Charles's later pieces may be weaker than his earlier work.[18] There might be some truth in this because after 1913 the company seems to have taken a downturn, appearing only infrequently in the trade journals. The next major mention appears in June of 1917, when Towse reported, "It will surprise a lot of furniture folks to hear that the Stickley & Brandt Chair Co. has discontinued the manufacture of mission furniture and gone into something else."[19] A year later, the company went into receivership and declared bankruptcy.[20] It would seem that Charles and Gustav were both having problems with bankruptcy at about the same time. Charles never joined the Associated Cabinet Makers simply because his own financial troubles would have been a further drain during difficult times. Despite Towse's comment that folks might be surprised to find that Stickley & Brandt had ceased production of mission furniture, such a move would have been long overdue since changes in style had started much earlier. Charles introduced his Arts & Crafts line just as the first signs of change were taking place. He was successful for a number of years but does not seem to have adapted to the newer styles quickly enough, and problems were bound to ensue.

By 1919, the company building was leased as a secondary base of operations by the Levinson Manufacturing Company, makers of bedroom chairs, rockers, and period dining chairs. It was headed by Charles Hall as president and Henry B. Lacey as vice president. Both men had been offi-

18. Two of the better authorities on restoration and construction of Arts & Crafts furniture, Paul Horan of Cambridge, Massachusetts, and Bill Lower of Ithaca, New York, agree that the later pieces, with the branded signature, seem to be weaker in design and construction.

19. John Towse, "On the Road," *Furniture World*, 19 June 1917, 28.

20. "Business Troubles," *Furniture World*, 9 May 1918, 46.

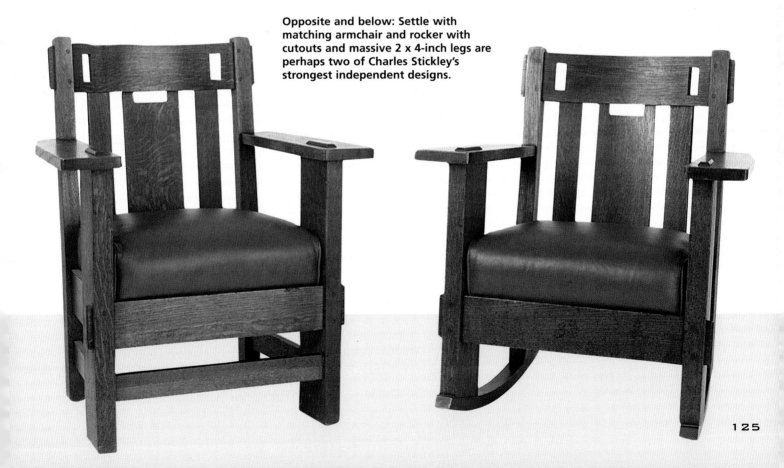

Opposite and below: Settle with matching armchair and rocker with cutouts and massive 2 x 4-inch legs are perhaps two of Charles Stickley's strongest independent designs.

Stickley & Brandt Chair Company factory in Binghamton, New York, just after the purchase of the plant by the Levinson Mfg. Co., the *Furniture World*, January 21, 1918.

cers for many years in the old Stickley & Brandt Chair Company and apparently took over the management of the branch plant until its demise in 1925. However, Charles Stickley was not to be involved in the furniture business again. He died in 1927, leaving the homestead to his widow and daughter.[21]

Charles Stickley lived his life, for the most part, at the center of where the Stickley/Brandt clan had been since they emigrated from Germany at the turn of the nineteenth century. Remaining at home, he had taken advantage of the family prestige in the area to build a local company that would trade on a national scale. Yet, in the larger microcosm of the American furniture industry, he remained a typical manufacturer and retailer. Throughout his life, Charles maintained contact with his brothers, often doing business with them, and certainly obtaining ideas from them for his own Arts & Crafts line.

In passing judgment on his work, one might agree with Bruce Johnson's 1962 assessment. Johnson indicated that David Cathers' earlier "blanket dismissal" of Charles Stickley's work as shabby might be premature. He also pointed out that Charles's work may suffer in comparison to Gustav's, but "no apology need be made for his workmanship."[22] The Arts & Crafts work of Charles Stickley has found favor with many collectors today for being solid and at times innovative. One would suspect that in the early years after 1909, Charles's brothers in Syracuse gave him their full support. With what we now know about Charles's work, we would add that although it might often appear to be inconsistent in its design and construction, there is virtue to be found in many of his pieces. More importantly, there are pieces that certainly rate with the work of L. & J. G. Stickley and Stickley Brothers. And there are those distinctively innovative chairs that are clearly a credit to

21. The purchase of the plant is discussed in "Levinson Mfg. Co. Expands," *Furniture World*, 21 November 1918, 11. The city directories continue to list Hall and Lacey as officers in the company until 1925, when the company disappears from the city directories. Strangely enough the company continues to be listed in the city directories as The Stickley-Brandt Furniture Company until 1925. Perhaps this may have been part of the lease arrangement. It is also rather strange that Schuyler Brandt remained listed as president of the company until 1917 in the city directories, in spite of the fact that he died in 1913.

22. Johnson, *Guide*, 106.

L. & J. G. Stickley factory, Fayetteville, NY, about 1910.

the Stickley clan and Charles's own name. These pieces are often unique but, as a body of work, do not offer us a widely imitated American style.

LEOPOLD AND JOHN GEORGE STICKLEY: THE SURVIVOR AND THE SALESMAN

Leopold Stickley was the last of the Stickley brothers to form his own company, but his union with John George Stickley would bring about a stroke of marketing genius. Although Leopold and John George had been involved with all of their brothers to one degree or another from 1890 onward, they did not establish their joint firm until the Arts & Crafts movement was well underway. Therefore, they were able to bring extensive training and an enormous amount of expertise into their new firm. Their practical experience and understanding of Arts & Crafts design would pay rich dividends in the longevity, success, and influence of the company.

Throughout the period between 1890 and the beginning of the new century, Leopold was involved in a number of leadership positions and associated closely with all of his brothers. In 1890 he worked with Charles in Binghamton as the factory foreman and left a year later with Gustav to become foreman of the furniture shop in the state prison. When Gustav opened his plant in Eastwood, Leopold began to work there, again as foreman. In 1895, he shows up in the Grand Rapids city directory associated with Albert Stickley and David Myers in Stickley & Myers, Boiler Purifiers.[23] David Cathers has indicated that in 1898 and 1899 Leopold was back in Binghamton working for Charles again. At some point during 1899, he returned to Syracuse to become foreman for Gustav and eventually became a stockholder and a member of his board of

23. *City Directories: R. L. Polk & Co. 1896 Grand Rapids City Directory* (Grand Rapids, MI: The Grand Rapids Directory Company, 1034).

directors. Thus, by 1900, Leopold had amassed an extensive amount of experience and was ready to strike out on his own.

In the meantime, John George had spent the period between 1890 and 1900 representing Stickley Brothers and working with Albert. In his work with this company, John George had obtained extensive sales experience. In 1899, he moved to New York and continued to represent Stickley Brothers at its New York offices. However, by 1901, he was no longer listed as vice president of Stickley Brothers and had resigned his position with the firm. Despite this, John George's move to New York would turn out to be fortuitous for himself and Leopold.

24. Letter from Leopold Stickley to F. A. Arwine, 8 September 1902, Winterthur Library, Joseph Downs Collection, 76x101.2356.

Frontispiece from Russmore catalogue published by The Tobey Furniture Co., Chicago, IL, 1903. The same drawing appears in the 1902 catalog.

Although the trade journals indicated that in February of 1902 Leopold had broken off connections with Gustav Stickley, he remained on Gustav's board of directors until he submitted his letter of resignation, dated September 8, 1902.[24] The letter was printed on stock that noted the new company shop mark as "The Onondaga Cabinet Shops." The words surrounded a cedar tree, perhaps serving to emphasize their specialization at the time in cedar pieces. However, the stock was also imprinted with "L. & J. G. Stickley, Fayetteville, N.Y." The payroll records of Gustav Stickley's firm indicate that

25. E-mail to the authors from David Cathers, December 2001.

26. Cathers has pointed out in a personal note that "Leopold worked for Gustav in Eastwood starting sometime in 1899 and in all of 1900 and 1901. His last full month of employment with Gustav was December 1901, but he continued to draw some pay until January 23, 1902. The payroll Ledger is located at Henry Francis DuPont Winterthur Library, Department of Archives, 76x101.11. John Knaus remained in the position of foreman until he and Fred Arwine joined John's brothers to establish the ill-fated Craftstyle company in 1906. See Michael E. Clark and Jill Thomas-Clark, "Gus Meets L. & J. G: Craftstyle," *Style 1900*, February 1997, 16-18 for a record of the establishment and demise of Craftstyle.

27. Donald Davidoff, *Innovation and Derivation*, 27. Davidoff's reference for the loan is based on an interview with Mildred Stickley (Gustav's daughter) done by Robert Judson Clark.

28. Donald Davidoff, *Innovation and Derivation*, 29.

although Leopold remained on the board, he was only employed through January of 1902.[25] His resignation was accepted and John Knaus, the current foreman, was named to the board of directors.[26] According to tradition, Leopold purchased the factory in Fayetteville with a loan from Gustav.[27] Thus, Leopold and John George were in business together by early 1902.

Donald Davidoff has suggested that Leopold could have already been making furniture by 1901. As previously noted, he provided evidence that in 1901, Leopold completed Gustav Stickley's contract with the Tobey Furniture Company and maintained a close ongoing relationship with George Clingman, the company's president, for a number of years. He linked Leopold's early work to the Tobey Furniture Company through drawings found in the Fayetteville factory and the 1902 Tobey Furniture Company catalog showing the Russmore line.[28]

Our own survey of the subsequent 1903 Russmore catalog reveals that much of the line is identical to the early Onondaga Shop line. The attic yielded several renderings of the new furniture line along with some other

Rocker, similar to model 110, and plant stand, model 325, both of rough-hewn green cedar, Onondaga Shops, about 1902–1906.

lines. They were annotated with various furniture company names such as John Wanamaker, Jordan Marsh, and Paine Furniture. Davidoff has specifically shown that one drawing is marked Tobey Furniture Company and is identical to a piece in Tobey's revised 1901 catalog of New Furniture. However, as Cathers has noted, if Leopold did begin making furniture, it is not clear where he would have made it. At this point, the evidence for the 1901 date remains inconclusive.[29] If Leopold completed the furniture contract, he would have had to make it in Gustav's Eastwood plant in 1901 or the Fayetteville plant in 1902.

Davidoff also points out that Tobey's 1902 Russmore line is directly connected to Leopold's work through a 1902 Russmore catalog found at Winterthur. He notes that the cedar pieces in the line "reveal an almost one-to-one correspondence with identical pieces produced both in oak and rough-hewn cedar by the L. & J. G. Stickley Co."[30] The 1902 date is both plausible and probable for the association between the two, and Davidoff is probably correct. This is certainly supported by the 1903 Russmore catalog, in which the majority of the furniture is from the Onondaga Cabinet Shop line. Davidoff also points out that evidence in the old factory links the early work of L. & J. G. Stickley to the other furniture companies as well:

The pattern that emerges suggests that Leopold imitated Gustav's original business strat-

29. Cathers, *Furniture*, 76.

30. Ibid.

egy and secured contracts from a variety of furniture companies to manufacture their furniture. Thus, in spite of not producing original designs, Leopold became an important force in the production of mission-style furniture. He could therefore secure a toehold in the furniture industry with minimal financial risk.[31]

31. Ibid.

No doubt, there was an early period for Leopold and John George's Onondaga Cabinet Shops during which they probably produced work for various furniture firms. However, the production of such early furniture does not preclude it being of their own independent design. Firms such as John Wanamaker, Jordan Marsh, and the Paine Furniture Company were department stores with catalogs selling furniture from various makers under their names, much as Tobey had done with Gustav Stickley. Producing furniture for various furniture stores and/or concerns was quite common during the period.

Although L. & J. G. Stickley more than likely produced many of the pieces in the Russmore line, it does not mean that they were producing pieces designed by someone else. Cathers has pointed out that in February of 1902, one trade journal announced the creation of the new L. & J. G. Stickley company and that it would make "rustic cedar furniture." Tobey trademarked the name of "Russmore" in January of 1903, although the furniture had been in production since May of 1902.[32] In November of 1902, a note appeared from John Towse indicating that more than the cedar pieces were in production and that a significant number of pieces were being sold to a number of furniture stores. It reinforces not only the link with Tobey, but also the independence of the new company. On his visit, Towse was unable to find the name Onondaga Shops on the factory buildings. He said, "Instead it was just plain L. & J. G. Stickley."[33] Towse's description of the early Onondaga Shops concern is well worth noting at length. Towse continued:

32. See Cathers, *Furniture*, 90 for references to each of the articles in the various trade journals.

33. John Towse, "On the Road," *Furniture World*, 27 November 1902, 16.

> The two Stickley boys have quite a plant there and are already employing sixty workmen. "We are not making mission furniture nor Arts & Crafts," said Leo Stickley, "just plain, simple furniture and a few stores take all we can make." It is pretty hard to state the case more explicitly. This plain simple furniture is made from chestnut and is fumed and oiled or stained green. They make a dining room suit and furniture for the library and living room. Quite a variety of it. The firm will get further away from the conventional furniture next season by essaying a line of unique clock mantels, hanging and standing clocks, and will also have a line of framed pictures. During the year the firm made a line of summer furniture from native cedar, showing the natural facing of the log. This had a good run and will be continued next year with additions. The Sticklevs are using a great many calf skins in their work, and it is noteworthy that the treatment of these skins is peculiarly their own. Looks as though Leo and George were building up a successful manufacturing business, and they will do it by getting out of the rut. There are now four separate-and distinct Stickley concerns and all the Stickley brothers are principals.[34]

34. Ibid.

The description states Leopold's early approach to the design of furniture and the success of his first

Chestnut china cabi-
net, model 605,
about 1902–1906.
This model first
appears in the 1902
Russmore Furniture
catalog and contin-
ues in the subse-
quent Onondaga
Shops catalogs.

Gustav Stickley oak bookcase, model 512, about 1901.

Chestnut bookcase, model 317, about 1903–1906. This model appears in the 1903 Russmore catalog and the subsequent Onondaga Shops catalogs.

year in business. He separated himself from pure Mission or Arts & Crafts to make plain simple furniture. In 1904 advertisements, it was referred to as "Arts & Crafts and simple furniture built on mission lines" and tied the company to the Arts & Crafts movement.[35] By 1914, as tastes began to change, the L. & J. G. Stickley catalog text emphasized the modernity of the furniture being created and "built in a scientific manner" not following "the traditions of a bygone day."[36] Furthermore, it advertised the company as "makers of the simple and entirely American type of furniture."

The Towse quote also indicates that by the end of 1902, Leopold and John George had a significant operation and were producing a variety of items for the dining room, library, and living room. They had a good-sized work force and expanded the line into several areas. They were already noted for their leatherwork, which, in the future, would become a useful selling point in the construction of their furniture. Towse's final statement announced that all the brothers were working in the trade and in four separate Stickley-owned firms. As a family together but separate, they represented a microcosm of the furniture industry. The firm of L. & J. G. Stickley was the new addition.

By early 1904, when the company incorporated, a new active phase had begun for the Onondaga Cabinet Shops. The line was based on the early developments of the period in between 1902 and 1903 as echoed by Towse. The first advertisement that appeared in the January 1904 *Upholstery Dealer and Decorative Furnisher* held to a simple note of L. & J. G. Stickley as the company's identification. It reported the brothers as "cabinet makers and leather workers" who made "simple furniture" and also had "a line of Framed Posters, Plate, and Pipe Racks, on the line of Arts & Crafts." In the April advertisement, the original name, The Onondaga Cabinet Shops, was shortened to Onondaga Shops for the first time. It also announced that a catalog had been issued.[37]

These early pieces, found in the 1904 catalog, were more than likely the culmination of the work developed and designed between 1902 and 1903. As Donald Davidoff has shown, they demonstrate an affinity with the design work of Gustav Stickley, but they also indicate experimentation and derivations that expanded Gustav's vocabulary of design. Davidoff has best summed up the early work in this way:

> Comparison with Gustav's work shows that Leopold's work during this Onondaga Shops period was often derivative and imitative. At times when Leopold did make design changes the results were crude or ungainly compared to Gustav's finely proportioned achievements.
>
> Occasionally, however, their designs built upon, strengthened or even improved upon Gustav's designs. . . . Sometimes, as when Onondaga Shops either created pieces not in Gustav's repertoire or departed innovatively from his line, they triumphed.[38]

As support for the comparison, he points to a series of items including a model 370 and model 374 desk, a model 684 china cabinet, and a model 609 serving table. He comments that they "incorporated shoe feet and an architectural approach to expressed structure quite distinct from equivalent forms that Gustav produced."[39] He continues by pointing out an early model 73 settle that reduces the form to its most basic structure. When placed next to the Gustav equivalents, the architectural quality

35. Advertisements in *Upholstery Dealer and Decorative Furnisher*, January and April, 1904.

36. *The Work of L. & J. G. Stickley*, 1.

37. Cathers, *Furniture*, 77. Identifies the catalog as being "presumably a reference to Handmade Furniture from the Onondaga Shops" and reprinted by Turn of the Century Editions, 1982, revised 1989.

38. Davidoff, *Innovation and Derivation*, 30.

39. Ibid.

Magazine rack, model 47, derived from Gustav Stickley magazine stand, model 79, about 1909.

40. Ibid., 71.

41. Tobey Furniture Company, *Some Designs in Mission furniture For Sale by The Tobey Furniture Co. Chicago*, (James Bayne Co. Grand Rapids). Original owned by the authors.

clearly differentiates them.

The newer pieces also carry through on many of the basic qualities of the earlier Onondaga forms while showing expansion and innovation on older Gustav Stickley forms. The early wooden knobs, chamfered backs, and an architectural emphasis are characteristic construction features of the early Onondaga work. The features often relate directly to their Gustav Stickley counterparts while extending it in different ways. For example, the model 103 chestnut bookcase of Onondaga Shops can be compared to Gustav Stickley's model 512 oak bookcase. The Onondaga work looks much the same in its form. However, the full-length pinned door and the solid chamfered backboard and sides with posts rather than slab construction give it an architectural solidity that differentiates it from Gustav's form. Davidoff finds that the tapering later forms, like the model 47 magazine stand, have an affinity with the Viennese Secessionist style.[40] Interestingly, model 47, as well other forms, have identical earlier counterparts in the Onondaga Shops catalog. Model 47 is virtually the same as the model 346 in this catalog. A number of pieces, like the stand, appear in the first catalog and were continued until the end of L. & J. G. Stickley's Arts & Crafts production.

The objects shown in the catalog and subsequent sketchbook are all Arts & Crafts in design and remain focused on pieces for the dining room, library, and living room. The catalog introduction points out that the pieces are not chestnut but "carefully selected oak, with a dull wax finish." However, the customer may send for "samples of the different finishes of both wood and leather." By the summer of 1904, L. & J. G. Stickley followed up its advertisement campaign and new catalog by exhibiting in Grand Rapids for the first time.

The exhibit in Grand Rapids that summer marked the official entrance of The Onondaga Shops into the furniture world. It was now a rising star to be reckoned with in Grand Rapids. A recently discovered Tobey Furniture Company catalog entitled *Some Designs in Mission Furniture For Sale by The Tobey Furniture Co. Chicago* reinforces the new independence of Leopold and John George.[41] This work is almost an exact reproduction of the Onondaga Shops catalog in layout design and in the reference numbers given to the furniture. It includes a number of new pieces including the model 619 China Cabinet and model 405 table along with other pieces such as the model 742 Daybed that had appeared in all the earlier "Russmore" catalogs by Tobey. David Cathers has pointed out that the date for the catalogs to 1904 can be reasonably ascertained. The proof lies in the appearance of the model 405 Table in both of them. This table first appears in an ad in the April 1904 issue of the *Upholstery*

Dealer and Decorative Furnisher.[42] It does not appear in the other earlier Tobey catalogs and appears in these two for the first time. Cathers has concluded and we agree that it is clear that "L. & J. G. Stickley was selling on its own and also acting as an unacknowledged subcontractor to Tobey even after incorporating in February 1904." Although unacknowledged by George Clingman's company, the furniture line is no longer incorporated under Tobey's "Russmore" line as it was before. This independence would call for growth and recognition for the company.

According to John Towse in the *Furniture World*, the firm showed again in January of 1905 at the winter exhibition with an expanded line of over 200 pieces and by March 1 had issued another "very fine catalog."[43] Towse reported that L. & J. G. Stickley continued to state that its line was neither Arts & Crafts nor Mission, but "simple furniture on mission lines." He also pointed out that "they make

Above: Oak server, model 641, and oval oak tray by Onondaga Shops, about 1905.

Below: Oak sideboard and rectangular oak mirror by Onondaga Shops, about 1905.

42. In a note (April 14, 2002) to the authors David Cathers has pointed out these comparisons and conclusions.

43. John Towse, "Notes," *Furniture World*, 2 February 1905, 30. Cathers in *Furniture*, 79, presumes this to be "Some Sketches of Furniture Made at the Onondaga Shops," reprinted, in Stephen Gray, ed., *The Mission Furniture of L. & J. G. Stickley* (New York: Turn of the Century Editions, 1989).

Left: Detail of carved decoration on leg of model 618 dining table.

Above: L. & J. G. Stickley five-leg dining table, model 618, with carved decoration on legs.

all of their trimmings, also prepare all skins for upholstering and decoration, and make the cushions." The company had grown considerably and rapidly. Throughout 1905, it continued to expand its line into numerous other areas. L. & J. G. Stickley was soon producing various window treatments, as well as other Arts & Crafts linens and home decorations that were displayed in a cottage near the factory and in the new sales rooms in New York managed by John George.[44]

The following year of 1906 was a transitional one for the expanding company, as it adopted a new name and patented a new seat. At some point in 1906, the firm issued its last Onondaga Shops catalog. At the exhibition in Grand Rapids, it adopted the new "Handcraft" furniture name, symbolized by a new label with a red carpenter's hand-clamp.[45] Importantly, Donald Davidoff found, in the old L. & J. G. Stickley factory, a 1906 Onondaga Shops catalog containing various photographs tipped into the back with 1906 Onondaga catalog numbers. These photos indicate L. & J. G. Stickley's experiments with a spindle line of furniture just a year after Gustav Stickley had introduced his line. The catalog also shows an attempt at creating some pieces with low-relief carving. Although most of the known pieces seem to have come from the basement of the old factory in Fayetteville, pieces do continue to surface in the marketplace, however rarely. To what extent these pieces ever became full production items remains unknown.

In 1907, the company continued to expand. The Handcraft name and logo were registered with the patent office. This symbol and name would remain in use until 1912, when a rectangular yellow decal containing the words "The Work of L. & J. G. Stickley" replaced it. During this latter period, it appears that the company would occasionally brand its work with these words as well.

44. Ibid.

45. Cathers feels that this is the salesman's catalog in *Early L. & J. G. Stickley Furniture From Onondaga Shops to Handicraft*, ed. Donald A. Davidoff and Robert L. Zarrow, reprint (Mineola, NY: Dover Publications, 1992). The salesman retail plates from about 1909 for Handcraft furniture by L. & J. G. also appear in this reprint.

■ ■

**Onondaga Shops
Morris chair with side
panels carved with a
tobacco leaf motif,
about 1906–1909.**

Design for a dining room by L. & J. G. Stickley originally published in the 1906 Handcraft catalog.

Donald Davidoff and Robert Zarrow found various other artifacts in the old Stickley factory that indicate a design evolution in the years between the 1906 catalog and the creation of a set of retail plates, or salesman's drawings, which Zarrow dates to about 1909. However, there is evidence that between 1907 and 1909, at least two sets of these retail plates were issued, raising the possibility that some of the furniture designs were produced earlier than 1909. There is an important note in the March 1907 issue of *The Decorative Furnisher* that describes the 1907 retail plates:

> We have received from L. & J. G. Stickley their new catalogue, which is both unique and artistic. It is a new box, 9 1/2 x 7 1/2 inches, and 1 1/2 inches deep, filled with perhaps 150 loose sheets. Each sheet has printed upon it an excellent crayon drawing of one or two pieces of furniture made by the factory, the result being more "lifelike" than the ordinary factory catalogue. To improve the appearance a colored line is drawn around each sheet, indented at the corner to receive the name, number and description of each piece. The printing is well done, a good quality paper is used, and total result is artistic.[46]

46. "Special Notice," *The Decorative Furnisher*, March 1907, 57.

There are additional notes in this trade publication, attesting to the firm's growth and expansion in 1907. In January, the same trade catalog reported that Leopold and John George had enlarged their factory, thereby increasing its capacity, and were making "furniture for every room in the house, bedroom excepted, and bedroom furniture is also made, on order."[47] In April, they announced that the company was producing "clocks to match their furniture." In June, they noted that they were doing draperies of "Handcraft Canvas and Russian Crash" that were stenciled and done with appropriate "touches of hand embroidery." As David Cathers pointed out, by December of 1907, a full catalog with approximately 300 illustrations was advertised in the *Furniture Trade Review*.[48]

The breadth of this new Handcraft line was illustrated in color in the company's 1907 catalog, and one of these illustrations appears in the February 1908 *Furniture Record*. The *Furniture Record* shows a living room completely outfitted with L. & J. G. Stickley pieces and done in a style that Leopold considered appropriate for his modern furniture. A clock that looks similar to one designed by Peter Hansen in 1909 appears on the mantel. The room is dominated by a massive Handcraft model 222 settle facing a model 462 Morris chair—their weight balanced by a model 522 library table. Other Handcraft accoutrements fill the room. However, as noted by the trade, it is the harmony of

Design for a living room by L. & J. G. Stickley originally published in the 1906 Handcraft catalog, the *Grand Rapids Furniture Record*, February 1908.

47. "L. & J. G. Stickley," *The Decorative Furnisher*, January 1907, 60.

48. Cathers, *Furniture*, 91.

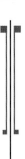

all the elements that attracts attention. The table, covered in green leather, blends with the matching upholstery and the fumed oak of the furniture. It is tasteful, uncluttered and welcoming. The same color scheme is repeated in the dining room illustration. However, instead of a fumed oak treatment, the wood is stained a green color that contrasts with the golden walls and patina of the copper trimmings on the sideboard. Although our eye is drawn to the blue-gray tiled fireplace, the warmth of the hearth in the living room, and the centrality of the table in the dining room, the emphasis appears to be placed on the furniture rather than the total environment, as is evoked in the Gustav Stickley images from 1903 and 1904. Nevertheless, in all the renderings, the images evoke the importance of the home as a place for practical, simple living.

L. & J. G. Stickley oak-paneled Prairie settle, model 220, about 1915.

A new set of retail drawings appeared in 1909 that included "bedroom furnishings," and another comprehensive catalog appeared in 1910. The *Furniture Trade Review* noted in December of 1909:

L. & J. G. Stickley produced a line for fall which was deemed by their customers and the trade generally the consummation of the best efforts that have been put forth along the lines of the well known style of furniture for which this house has achieved such high repute. But new life appears in the spring line, which will be shown by J. George Stickley [in] . . . Grand Rapids. It will be worth the while of any dealer to get the handsome plates

49. "New York State and Pennsylvania," *The Furniture Trade Review*, December 1909, 104.

which have recently been issued by the firm, one showing everything for the library, another a complete assortment for the dining room, another for the bedroom and a fourth for the living room.[49]

The new 1909 spring line expanded to the entire house, offering a more comprehensive line of furniture for the consumer. The difference between the retail plates for 1907 and 1909 would appear to be the absence of furniture for the bedroom in the 1907 set. Because of this omission, we can assume that the spindle line was in limited production by 1907 following the photos tipped into the Onondaga Shops catalog of 1906. In either case, these two sets of plates, the company's rapid expansion, and the subsequent comprehensive Handcraft catalogs issued in 1908 and 1910, represent the rapid maturation and growth of the L. & J. G. Stickley furniture line. This maturation came at a time when the Arts & Crafts movement had reached its high point in America, and a slow shift in taste had begun. By this time, all of the Stickley brothers were at their apex producing Arts & Crafts furniture and accessories.

50. Cathers, *Furniture*, 84.

51. *Trow's General Directory of the Boroughs of Manhattan and Bronx City of New York*, vol. CXXV for year ending August 1, 1912 (New York: Trow Directory, Printing and Bookbinding Company, 1912), 1522. Gustav's offices were at 41 West 34th Street. L. & J. G.'s office was in room 815, while the Stickley Brothers' office was in room 812.

In 1910, Leopold and John George opened "a four-story building in Grand Rapids with a large showroom. . . . Also that year they moved their New York City offices to 47 W. 34th Street."[50] The 34th Street office was up the street from Gustav and, in 1912, just a few rooms down from Stickley Brothers.[51] Within two years, Leopold and John George had issued a supplemental catalog, "The Work of L. & J. Stickley," which would carry their designs with their Prairie school influence to full maturity and breathe fresh air into the fading fashion of the Arts & Crafts movement.

Donald Davidoff's comments about the earlier transitional prototypes and the culmination of the new direction in the plates and catalogs are particularly appropriate here. He notes:

> The development of these prototypical pieces marked a new maturity for the work of L. & J. G. Stickley and a pivotal turn in the commercial Arts & Crafts aesthetic. The new designs exemplified a fresh approach whose roots could be stylistically traced to three sources—the Prairie style of Frank Lloyd Wright, the European Reform Movement espoused by the Viennese architect-designers and the English Arts & Crafts masters such as Voysey, Mackmurdo and Grimson. The synthesis of these disparate influences revitalized the simple mission style and pushed the firm of L. & J. G. Stickley into a new prominence in the marketplace. Though the full realization of this new aesthetic would only reach fruition over the next several years, the work reproduced in the Handcraft retail plates does illustrate the roots of these designs.[52]

52. Davidoff, "Introduction," *Early L & J. G.*, xii.

The support for his assertions rests on a number of illustrations attached to the Onondaga Shops catalog, which show the transitions in design of Leopold's spindle chairs and the later designs for his 1912 Prairie-style settles and chairs inspired by Wright's designs for the Robie House in 1909.

Much of the innovation exhibited during these years was a result of the employment of Peter Hansen as Leopold's designer. Hansen had worked for Gustav for a few years beginning in 1904.

According to Davidoff, after leaving Gustav, Hansen was employed in 1909 "by Leopold to be both shop foreman and chief designer."[53] However, some doubt has been raised as to the validity of the 1909 date as the definitive hiring point. Hansen was employed by L. & J. G. Stickley until the 1940s. He died in 1947.[54] The longer corbels seen on chairs, the graceful arches and overhanging beveled tops that appear on the furniture were probably influenced by him, as they are natural extensions to the work he did for Gustav Stickley. By the end of 1909, the second set of retail plates was published and issued to dealers. Much of this work reflects the Prairie school movement and that of the Viennese and English influences seen earlier in some of the designs by Albert Stickley.

It is in these later pieces designed by Hansen for L. & J. G. Stickley that we find a new expression of the American Arts & Crafts movement offered to the consumer. The clocks and the Prairie school furniture in the line are the best illustrations. The clocks created by Hansen demonstrate his familiarity with work of C. F. A. Voysey and the German designer F. C. Morawe. However, as Davidoff has pointed out, a similar Voysey clock relies on its polychrome finish and the Morawe example on carving to enhance the work. The L. & J. G. Stickley clock designed by Hansen is simpler and emphasizes form and architectural structure rather than decoration, which links it directly to the American movement and Gustav's initial thesis on American style and structure.

Between 1910 and 1912, the work of Leopold and John George matured and, in some cases, expanded upon the work of Gustav Stickley. The designs for the spindled and paneled settles and chairs were not in Gustav's, Charles's, or Albert's vocabularies. The differences lie in the emphasis on the horizontal planes of the Prairie school rather than on the verticality of Gustav's work.

53. Ibid., xiii.

54. In an E-mail to the authors, David Cathers notes that he feels Peter Hansen was "hired before 1909" and was the only designer for L. & J. G. Stickley until the 1940s. His assertion is based on an interview with Louise Stickley and former factory employees.

Left: L. & J. G. Stickley shelf clock, model 85, about 1910, designed by Peter Hanson.

Right: Gustav Stickley shelf clock, about 1913.

Davidoff sums up the Prairie school's design concepts:

> The design emphasizes the interplay of elementary horizontal planes with massive vertical piers to indicate its earth-bound quality. The eye should be allowed long open vistas, so narrow vertical spindles create screened spaces without impeding the view. Furthermore, dominant horizontal elements with vertical accents break up solid planes into eye-catching patterns. The eye is thus always drawn along the horizontal axis.[55]

55. Davidoff, *Innovation and Derivation*, 34.

There are imitations of Gustav's spindle chairs in Leopold's work, but vertical slats often replace Gustav's spindles. Leopold achieves the same verticality but with a heavier chair that harks back to an earlier aesthetic in Gustav's design. The model 812 L. & J. G. Stickley tall-back dining chair can be directly compared to Gustav's well-known and currently reproduced #374 spindle dining chair. However, the solidity of the form of Leopold's Handcraft chair presents a totally different feel from the light and vertical emphasis of the Craftsman piece by Gustav.

When they issued their next catalog around 1914, the times of change were well underway, and Leopold and John George seem to have been slower to adapt than either Charles, Albert, or Gustav. By 1910, Charles was producing Jacobean Revival in addition to his Arts & Crafts line. In 1913, Albert had already introduced his Manor line, and by 1915 even Gustav's failing company was beginning to look in other directions. With the changes in design prevalent in the summer of 1916, Leopold began to make concessions. In that year, John Towse reported:

> . . . the [Stickley] boys are still building mission furniture and shipping a lot of it. And from what I have observed, they are going to continue to make oak mission furniture indefinitely, but there will be something new for fall, something original; not mission, not period, furniture entirely different from that which has kept the plant going for fourteen years. The wood will be a native wood. The finish, a finish never seen before.[56]

56. John Towse, "On the Road," *Furniture World*, 8 June 1916, 6.

In August, Towse described the new line as an "antique proposition" based on a collection of "treasures and heirlooms" that Leopold had gathered from around Onondaga County. All of the reproduction antiques would be finished with a Chromewald finish. This was the finish that Gustav had developed for his final furniture line, a product of the merger of the two companies as Gustav's faded in 1916. Interestingly, Towse concluded that "in addition to the antiques the Stickleys will make a line of Shaker chairs and rockers for 1917. These goods originated with the Shakers of Lebanon, N. Y. but have not been made in a long time."[57]

With the new line, and especially with the manufacture of the Shaker furniture, it seemed that the Stickley brothers had come full circle, back to their days with Brandt in Binghamton. But it was not to be. In 1916, Gustav, Leopold, and John George formed the Stickley Associated Cabinetmakers. The following year, Albert joined the other three brothers as a director in the short-lived company. Charles, the brother who stayed behind, did not take part.[58]

57. John Towse, "On the Road," *Furniture World*, 26 August 1916, 6.

58. Charles was having his own problems during this period. He stopped making Mission furniture in 1917 and declared bankruptcy in 1918. See the earlier notes on Charles Stickley in this chapter.

By 1918, the company had adopted a new label that combined the joiner compass of Gustav Stickley with the carpenter's hand-screw clamp of the Handcraft label—a symbolic link. By the end of the year, Gustav Stickley had left the company, and the brothers were separate again. Gustav retired to eventually live with his daughter Barbara Wiles in Syracuse, in the old family home on Columbus Street. He died in 1942 after what seems to have been a pleasant retirement in obscurity. John George died suddenly and unexpectedly in 1921, leaving Leopold to manage his company, while Albert continued on in Grand Rapids for a few more years until his retirement to Michigan's Upper Peninsula. Leopold issued one last catalog for the Handcraft and Craftsman line in 1922. It was filled with the standard pieces, and most of the copies never left the factory, probably because within a year he discontinued the line. He sold his remaining stock and turned to his Cherry Valley line of colonial reproductions, leaving others to carry on the manufacturing of Arts & Crafts lines.

In 1950, Leopold celebrated the fiftieth anniversary of the founding of the L. & J. G. Stickley Company. The event was punctuated by the debut of *The Story of A Developing Furniture Style*, a book published by the L. & J. G. Stickley Company and told from Leopold's point of view. The work vocalized in some depth the evolution of Leopold's Cherry Valley line of furniture. It told how the line had been developed from the settlers that made their homes near Albany, New York. It specified how "American Colonial furniture is . . . far from a single style" [59] and instead a combination

59. *The Story of a Developing Furniture Style* (Fayetteville, NY: The L. & J. G. Stickley Inc., 1950), 12.

60. Ibid. 10.

of various German, English, and Dutch influences while remaining American. The book defined style as "beauty adapted to the spirit of the times" and indicated that styles in furniture "in the main combine the features of design, comfort, construction, and utility which rich years of experience have proved most suitable." Yet, a style for Leopold had to conform "to the architecture and living habits of the modern home." [60] Supposedly, the Cherry Valley line had lived up to Leopold's expectations of an American style. For Leopold, the modern man of furniture and the surviving Stickley brother after sixty-plus years of making furniture, the emphasis was on the furniture and the object as it inhabits the space. It was not a way of life; it was not the art that is life. It was not built on an Arts & Crafts philosophy. Nevertheless, his approach was vital to the work and his role in the microcosm of what was the Stickley brothers. Leopold was a practical furniture maker, and his company survived as did the Stickley brothers' heritage.

After Leopold Stickley died in 1957, his family barely kept the company running. When Alfred and Aminy Audi purchased the firm in 1974, it employed only twenty-five people. By 1989, with the resurgence of the Arts & Crafts movement after the seminal Princeton exhibit in 1972, the Stickley name and the brothers were guaranteed a new success in its revival of furniture in the Arts & Crafts tradition.

Page from an undated L. & J. G. Stickley Cherry Valley Line catalog.

Opposite: L. & J. G. Stickley bow-arm Morris chair, model 406, about 1910, derivative of Gustav Stickley's bow-arm model 336 modified by Prairie school style.

Overleaf: Living room furnished with L. & J. G. Stickley reissue furniture.

The End of the Quest

The mythic proportions attached to the name Stickley based on the brothers' achievements in the decorative arts during the twentieth century are well deserved. Unfortunately, it is impossible to cover the distance their accomplishments have traveled in a comprehensive way. It is clear, however, that the span was covered through the contributions of all of the brothers, each bridging the way for the others at various times in their quest for an

American voice and their own individual voices. That pilgrimage began in the hills of northern Pennsylvania and spread throughout this nation and the world. As they traveled, they spoke collectively in a voice that echoed an American style in the decorative arts.

From their beginnings in the mid-1870s through the 1890s, all of the brothers learned their trade and forged a name for themselves in the furniture industry. It was during these years that Albert Stickley established himself not only as a major national figure but as an international one as well, by expanding his interest into England. It was there that he encountered the Arts & Crafts

Oak sideboard with wrought-iron hardware, about 1903. Produced by Gustav Stickley for the interior of his house on Columbus Avenue in Syracuse.

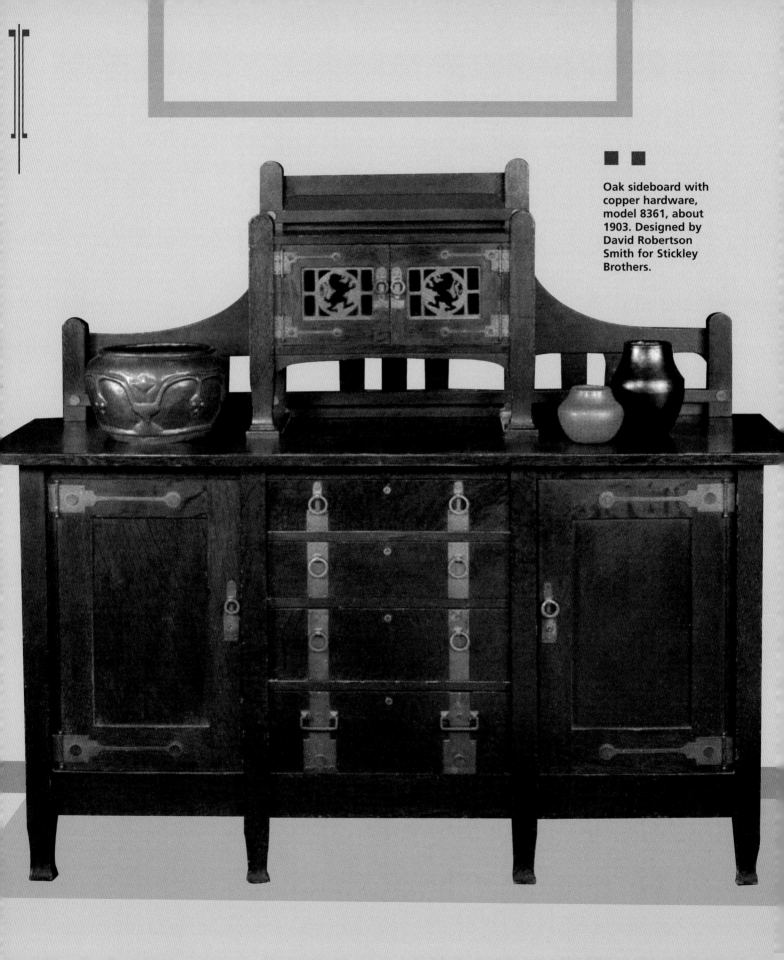

Oak sideboard with copper hardware, model 8361, about 1903. Designed by David Robertson Smith for Stickley Brothers.

movement and came to understand the new movements in the decorative arts in England and all of Europe. During these years Gustav Stickley also made the initial trips to England and Europe that influenced his groundbreaking work in 1900. The resulting experimentation of each of these brothers formed the style they would shape at the turn of the century. In turn, these styles would influence others. Albert and Gustav each drew upon many of the same sources, but the final product was distinctly different. Albert and his designers would show an innovative English and European design form but, as he admitted, they would not be the first to create an American form. In contrast, Gustav's trips, studies, and efforts led in different directions.

Charles Stickley was the brother who stayed at home. While an excellent manager and an above-average furniture maker, only for a brief period did he create an innovative form in the Arts & Crafts language. Otherwise, much of Charles's fashionable work was often derivative and imitative. He was neither a style maker nor a major force in design. Nevertheless, he remained a touchstone for the rest of the brothers simply because of his link to the base of the Stickley clan. Thus, Charles's contribution was also a part in the ongoing saga.

The youngest of the five brothers, John George, was primarily instrumental in purveying the beauty of his brothers' designs through his salesmanship for their companies. As he moved between each one of them as their spokesperson, he preached the vitality of the marketplace. It was a role that gave him a thorough understanding of the ebb and flow of the various styles that the public wanted. In one of his last letters to his brother Leopold, John George promoted Gustav's Chromewald furniture. In 1916, he wrote, " [Gustav's] line is a wonder. I have never seen such beautiful furniture and I think you would agree with me if you could see his show here."[1] In its own tragic way, John George's death in 1921 marked the end of the Stickley brother's active work in the Arts & Crafts movement.

John George's final partner and the only brother to survive to the end of the era was Leopold. Leopold's significance lies in that after following in his brothers' footsteps, he expanded the vocabulary of the design forms that Gustav had initially created. Perhaps even more importantly, Leopold was able to disseminate and expand on Gustav's creations. He was able to reach an even wider audience, thereby prolonging the American Arts & Crafts movement and its distinctive American style. Neither Leopold nor his brothers would realize what would become of Leopold's factory or the style they had produced.

This Charles Stickley sideboard is an imitation of L. & J. G. Stickley's model 734 sideboard. However, it differs from its prototype by the addition of a mirror and arched apron and rails.

1. Letter from John George Stickley to Leopold Stickley, 16 July 1916, cited in Davidoff, *Innovation and Derivation*, 42.

THE BIRTH OF AN AMERICAN STYLE

If an American style grew out of the Arts and Crafts movement that reflects both the principles of the movement and an American way of viewing it, we must look to the early work of Gustav Stickley and his thoughts on the subject. By 1901, Stickley had actually lived an idealized existence. Born into a harsh frontier life and developing a successful, entrepreneurial spirit, he identified with the Lincoln ideal. From these roots, in his role as director of design, he createed artistic forms that reflected what he perceived as the American style—a style based in structure. To find the correct form, one had to strip away the surface adornment, and he did that in its rawest form in his early work. Perhaps it is only that the massive model 2638 Eastwood Arm Chair, the often experimental model 2340 Bow Arm Morris Chair, or the frequently copied model 2342 Morris Chair from the years between 1901 and 1902 should be given that credit. Nevertheless, there are many of Gustav Stickley's objects from those years that deserve equal credit as icons of American style. In such forms lie much of what we see as idealized American culture as well as what we would like to be true in ourselves. Did Gustav borrow from other artistic sources? Yes, of course he did, but not in a spurious way. He interpreted those sources as any artist uses other various ious forms and ideas to take the quantum leap into an original style. In contrast to what Albert thought, Gustav did "for the American people what Boule did for the French, what the brothers Adam, Chippendale, Hepplewhite and Sheraton did for the English." Neither Albert, Charles, John George, nor Leopold created an American style—Gustav did.

Onondaga Shops oak sideboard, about 1905.

Opposite: Gustav Stickley Eastwood chair, model 2638, and seat, model 725, about 1901. Both objects were photographed in Gustav Stickley's home on Columbus Avenue.

For Gustav Stickley, the years after 1901 and 1902 were extensions of what had begun during those years. This was when Gustav's style was augmented by his designers, his brothers, and countless others that expanded, deviated, imitated, and innovated based on his first essential forms. However, Gustav would take the basic form and extend it into a lifestyle that was practical, and based on simple structure—a concept that obsessed him for the rest of his career. A turning point for him may well have been the viewing and understanding of the German exhibit at the World's Fair in St. Louis after his visit to Europe the year before. While others saw only furniture, Stickley saw an environment. He understood how furniture needed to be integrated into the environment of one's life. He had stated such ideas before, but now tried to put it into an American framework. His Craftsman homes and other dreams would follow. Many were not realized, but they would live on and remain an idealized American dream.

The remaining Stickley brothers—Albert, John George, Leopold, and Charles—played their parts as did others, and aided Gustav in the creation and extension of the style. Gustav's achievements should not overshadow the other brothers' accomplishments because without them, the style more than likely would not have been born and given a voice. One should not lose sight of the able

Left: Gustav Stickley Bow Arm
Morris chair, model 2342,
about 1901.

Right: Gustav Stickley Morris
chair, model 2340, about 1901.

designers and craftsmen that followed in the shadow of Gustav Stickley. Gustav and his brothers had a talent for surrounding themselves with very capable people who often brought out the best in those around them. Whether it was Gustav's work with Harvey Ellis and LaMont Warner, or Albert's work with David Robertson Smith and Timothy Conti, each of the brothers seemed to have that talent. Leopold and John George were an unbeatable team, but eventually they relied on the designs and ideas of Peter Hansen to extend their initial plans.

THE CONTINUING ARTS & CRAFTS STYLE

We should not overlook the work of countless others who continued this movement from the twentieth century well into the twenty-first. The Arts & Crafts style, as initially envisioned by Gustav Stickley, continued as an American form in the hands of others. In 1926, after Leopold had exhausted his Arts & Crafts stock, he turned his orders over to the J. M. Young and Sons Company of Camden, New York.[2] It was an appropriate move on Leopold's part. As we have shown in our own study of this firm, the J. M. Young Furniture Company consistently produced a line of Arts & Crafts furniture for a longer period than perhaps any other commercial firm in the United States. Well known for its quality craftsmanship, this small family business, founded in New York State in 1872 by a Scottish immigrant, left an enduring legacy in American decorative arts that lasted well into the twentieth century. Indeed, this firm continued to produce some Arts & Crafts pieces into the late 1940s and early fifties. The company did not fully cease production until 1979. Some of its work is equal to the best of the Stickley work and has been copied by today's artisans as well. The company's model 186 Morris chair, an early version of Gustav Stickley's model 352 Morris chair, came as both a rocker and a regular Morris chair, something Gustav never offered.

There were numerous other companies that produced imitations, derivations and innovations based on Gustav's and his brothers' work. In upstate New York, the interchange of ideas between employees and designers was incestuous. Quite literally, the area was covered with small companies that created various Arts & Crafts lines. Some companies, such as the Majestic Furniture Company of Mexico, New York[3] or the Quaint Art Company of Syracuse were small concerns that lived only an ephemeral existence,[4] while others were large concerns like the Frank Harden Company of Camden and McConnellsville, New York, which continues today as the current Stickley company does in Manlius, New York.[5] Similarly, there is work being done by countless smaller organizations and artists that continues to extend the voice of the American Arts & Crafts movement. Thus, at the turn of the twentieth century, Gustav and his brothers had initiated, developed, and extended an American style that reflected American culture. In doing so, they issued a challenge and an obligation for other artists and people to explore and build on what had been created. The formidable task that remains for us is to continue to answer the challenge and fulfill the obligation issued by the Stickley brothers.

2. Michael Clark and Jill Thomas-Clark, "Introduction," *J. M. Young Arts & Crafts Furniture* (Mineola, NY: Dover Publications, 1994), xi-xxvi.

3. Michael E. Clark and Jill Thomas-Clark, "The Majestic Furniture Company: Gus Meets Frank Lloyd Wright" *Style 1900*, May 1999, 21-25.

4. Michael E. Clark and Jill Thomas-Clark, "The Quaint Art Furniture Company of Syracuse, New York" *Style 1900*, August 1996, 12-14.

5. Michael E. Clark and Jill Thomas-Clark, "Is It Harden or The American Chair Manufacturing Company?" *Style 1900*, November 1996, 13-15.

Majestic Furniture Company massive sideboard
with hand-wrought copper hardware, about 1910.
This sideboard is a successful derivative of Gustav
Stickley's model 961.

IDENTIFYING THE STICKLEY BROTHERS' FURNITURE SHOP MARKS

All of the Stickley brothers utilized various paper labels, decals, and branded marks to identify and market their products. It has not been the purpose of this book to attempt to identify or date all of the brothers' various pieces. Others have given this subject detailed treatment and have offered precise instructions on how to identify and date their work by looking at the construction and the identifying shop marks.

Currently, the best work on identifying the furniture of Gustav Stickley and Leopold and John George Stickley by shop marks and construction is David Cathers's *Furniture of the American Arts and Crafts Movement* (Turn of the Century Editions, 1996). Cathers identifies approximately nine different labels that appeared both separately and together on Gustav Stickley's Arts & Crafts furniture between 1900 and 1916. The marks illustrated here follow his chronology. Most of these marks usually incorporated Gustav Stickley's joiner's compass and his motto "Als ik Kan." However, according to David Cathers, a plain gummed paper sticker of the type purchased at a five-and-ten-cent store with a handwritten inventory number has appeared on the 1900 New Furniture line that Stickley was retailing himself. There were other marks used prior to these on the Stickley and Simonds line, as well as the later cojoined label used by the Stickley Associated Cabinet Makers when most of the brothers later joined

GUSTAV STICKLEY

1. Tobey label, 1900. Used by the Tobey Furniture Company to mark Stickley "New Furniture."

2. Shop mark of a joiner's compass, early 1901. According to Cathers, there is no evidence that this mark was used on furniture.

3. Shop mark of a joiner's compass, 1901, published on the back cover of the *Craftsman*, volume 1, number 1. According to Cathers, no furniture with this mark has appeared.

4. Red decal, joiner's compass around the words "Als ik Kan" with "Stickley" in script enclosed in a rectangle, 1902–3. H: 1 to 2 1/2 inches.

together to form their own company. Cathers pictures the co-joined label in his section on the L. & J. G. Stickley Furniture Company along with the early Onondaga Shops, Handcraft, and the 1912 "Work of L. & J. G. Stickley" labels. Any possible earlier or later shop marks are not shown. However, Cathers has wisely cautioned against identifying any of the Stickley brothers' furniture by the marks alone, but urges that one "know the furniture first, and then look for marks as confirmation."

The shop marks of both Albert and Charles Stickley's companies are more problematic. Albert's company marks are very briefly treated in the introduction to *The 1912 Quaint Furniture Catalog* (Parchment Press, 1993), by Don Marek and Richard Widerman. Perhaps the best work to consult for identification of both these brothers' marks is Bruce Johnson's *Official Identification and Price Guide to Arts and Crafts* (House of Collectibles, 1992). Johnson's work gives a brief history of each company and some of the known marks associated with each of the brothers. Although his observations are not as comprehensive as Cathers's, we have followed his dates for Charles Stickley's marks and descriptions.

Albert's shop marks are difficult because all of the various paper and metal marks of this company appear from 1903 to 1918 or perhaps even later, making pieces difficult to date. All of the branded marks for Charles, Albert, and L. & J. G. first appear in and around 1913. The later branded marks of Albert and Charles are discussed but are not illustrated in any of the sources. As in the case of Gustav and L. & J. G., earlier labels do not appear for either Charles or Albert, although they more than likely existed.

We offer some sample renderings of known marks below; however, we advise each person to take the general advice of Cathers by studying the furniture and objects first. This can be done through examining the widely available reprinted catalogs and reading the descriptive passages in the mélange of available books and articles. The individual should then look for shop marks as a last resort, which may or may not exist due to the ephemeral nature of such signs.

5. Red decal, joiner's compass around the words "Als ik Kan" with "Stickley" in script below, all enclosed in a rectangle, 1902–4. H: 1 inch.

6. Decal, joiner's compass around the words "Als ik Kan" with "Gustav Stickley" in script below, 1904–6/7. H: 3/4 inch and 2 1/2 inches.

7. Red decal or sometimes black ink, variant of mark 6, 1905–12. H: 1 1/2 inches.

8. Black brand, joiner's compass around the words "Als ik Kan" with "Stickley" in script below, 1912–16. H: 1 1/4 inches.

Gustav Stickley seemingly began using paper labels in conjunction with the joiner's compass shop marks in 1905.

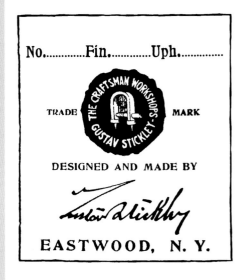

Paper label 1, 1905–7, printed in black ink on white paper and generally found in conjunction with no. 7. H: 2³/₄ x 3 inches.

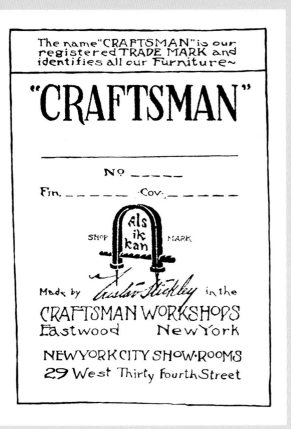

Paper label 2, 1907–12, printed on brown paper and generally found in conjunction with no. 7. H: 3 x 4³/₄ inches.

L. & J. G. STICKLEY

1. Rectangular Onondaga Shops decal, "The Onondaga Shops, L. & J. G. Stickley. Fayetteville, N.Y.," about 1904–6.

2. Oval brown paper label, "The Onondaga Shops" and a capital S, about 1904–6.

3. Red decal, handscrew with "L. & J. G. Stickley" printed on the jaws, 1906–12.

4. Red and yellow rectangular decal, "The Work of L. & J. G. Stickley," 1912–18.

CRAFTSMAN

TRADE MARKS REG'D   TM U.S. PATENT OFFICE

Stickley

THIS PASTER TOGETHER WITH MY DEVICE AND SIGNATURE (BRANDED) ON A PIECE OF FURNITURE STANDS AS MY GUARANTEE TO THE PURCHASER THAT THE PIECE IS MADE WITH THE SAME CARE AND EARNESTNESS THAT HAS CHARACTERIZED ALL MY EFFORTS FROM THE BEGINNING. AND IS MEANT TO IMPLY THAT I HOLD MYSELF RESPONSIBLE FOR ANY DEFECTS IN MATERIAL, WORKMANSHIP OR FINISH THAT MAY BE DISCOVERED BY THE PURCHASER EVEN AFTER THE PIECE HAS BEEN IN USE FOR A REASONABLE LENGTH OF TIME. AND THAT I WILL EITHER MAKE GOOD ANY DEFECTS OR TAKE BACK THE PIECE AND REFUND THE PURCHASE PRICE.

THIS PIECE WAS MADE IN MY CABINET SHOPS AT EASTWOOD, N. Y.

GUSTAV STICKLEY

Paper label 3, 1912–16, printed in blue ink on brown paper. H: 4 x 6 inches.

THE WORK OF L. & J. G. STICKLEY

5. Black branded mark, "The Work of L. & J. G. Stickley," 1912–18.

6. Round red and gold conjoined Handcraft and Craftsman decal, joiner's compass and handscrew with "Handcraft Craftsman" below and encircled by "Stickley / Syracuse & Fayetteville N.Y.," 1918.

CHARLES STICKLEY

1. Rectangular gold and red decal, "Stickley & Brandt Chair Company" with "Chas. Stickley" in script, "Genl. Mgr." below, 1909–ca. 1913.

2. Black branded mark, "Chas. Stickley" in script, about 1913–ca. 1918.

STICKLEY BROTHERS

1. Oval paper label, "Made By / Stickley Bros. Co. / Grand Rapids, Mich."

2. Brass tag or decal, "Quaint Furniture / Stickley Bros. Co. / Grand Rapids, Mich."

3. Black branded mark, "Stickley Bros. Co. / Grand Rapids."

ARTS & CRAFTS RESOURCES

AUCTION HOUSES

Butterfields
7601 Sunset Boulevard
Los Angeles, CA 90046
323.850.7500
220 San Bruno Avenue
San Francisco, CA 94103
415.861.7500
www.butterfields.com

Christie's
20 Rockefeller Plaza
New York, NY 10020
212.492.5485
info@christies.com
www.christies.com

Craftsman Auctions
333 North Main Street
Lambertville, NJ 08530
www.craftsman-auctions.com
Contacts:
Jerry Cohen
800.448.7828
aurora6@mindspring.com
John Fontaine
413.448.8922
fontaine@taconic.net
David Rago
609.397.9374
david@ragoarts.com

Skinner
The Heritage on the Garden
63 Park Plaza
Boston, MA 02116
617.350.5400
www.skinnerinc.com

Sotheby's
Twentieth-Century Decorative
Works of Art
1334 York Avenue
at 72nd Street
New York, NY 10021
212.606.7000
www.sothebys.com

Treadway Gallery/
John Toomey Gallery
Don Treadway
John Toomey
2029 Madison Road
Cincinnati, OH 45208
513.321.6742
513.871.7722 fax
info@treadwaygallery.com
www.treadwaygallery.com

DEALERS

Arts & Crafts Style
Pamela Witt
Mission Viejo, CA
949.472.0483

ASG Antiques
Leo Gallarano
Ann Gallarano
Route 2 Box 66
Berkeley Springs, WV 25411
304.258.4037
galarano@intrepid.net

Joyce Bennett
Rich Bennett
284 Ridge Road
Campbell Hall, NY 10916
845.496.5292
benjoy@frontiernet.net

Berkeley Bungalow
2508 San Pablo Avenue
Berkeley, CA 94702
510.981.9520
www.berkeleybungalow.com

Berman Gallery
136 N. Second Street
Philadelphia, PA 19106
Mailing address:
441 S. Jackson Street
Media, PA 19063
215.733.0707
www.bermangallery.com

Cathers & Dembrosky
Beth Cathers
43 East 10th Street
New York, NY 10003
212.353.1244

Circa 1910 Antiques
Jim and Jill West
7206 Melrose Avenue
Los Angeles, CA 90046
323.965.1910
317 N. El Camino Real
San Clemente, CA 92672
949.366.1510
west1910@pacbell.net
www.circa1910antiques.com

Classic Interiors & Antiques
Doug and Paula White
2042 N. Rio Grande Avenue #E
Orlando, FL 32804
407.839.0004
alauc@gateway.net

Jerry Cohen
Mission Oak Shop
109 Main Street
Putnam, CT 06260
860.928.6662
aurora@neca.com
www.artsncrafts.com

Dalton's
David Rudd
Debbie Goldwein Rudd
1931 James Street
Syracuse, NY 13206
315.463.1568
rudd@daltons.com
www.daltons.com

The Geoffrey Diner Gallery, Inc.
1730 21st Street NW
Washington, DC 20009
202.483.5005
202.483.2523 fax
mgd@dinergallery.com
www.dinergallery.com

Mark Eckhoff Antiques
Mark Eckhoff
P.O. Box 1116
Buckington, PA 18912
215.794.2774

Edwards Antiques and Collectibles
Cindy and Tom Edwards
Box 364
89 Hillsboro Street
Pittsboro, NC 27312
919.542.5649
antiques@emji.net

The Emporium
Cary Pasternak
1800 Westheimer
Houston, TX 77098
713.528.3808
www.the-emporium.com

Farmers and Merchants Gallery
Conrad Shields
Wes Miller
P.O. Box 615
Pilot Point, TX 76258
940.686.2396

Michael FitzSimmons
Decorative Arts
311 W. Superior Street
Chicago, IL 60610
312.787.0496
contact@fitzdecarts.com
www.fitzdecarts.com

Pearce Fox
162 N. Third Street
Philadelphia, PA 19106
610.688.3678
ei216@aol.com
www.foxmission.com

Gallery 532 Tribeca
142 Duane Street
New York, NY 10013
212.964.1282
www.gallery532.com

Raymond Groll
P.O. Box 421, Station A
Flushing, NY 11358
718.463.0050
grollmetal@aol.com

Heartwood
Don Marek
956 Cherry Street
Grand Rapids, MI 49506
616.454.1478

Hill House Antiques
276 S. Undermountain Road
(Route 41)
Sheffield, MA 01257
413.229.2374

JMW Gallery
Jim Messineo
Mike Witt
144 Lincoln Street
Boston, MA 02111
617.338.9097
mail@jmwgallery.com
www.jmwgallery.com

LifeTime Gallery
Robert Noble
7506 Santa Monica Boulevard
West Hollywood, CA 90046
323.939.7441
lifetimegallery@yahoo.com
www.lifetimegallery.com

George & Karin Look
608 Johnson Place
Alexandria, VA 22301
703.683.3871

Lower's Mission Furniture
Bill Lower
425 Floral Avenue
Ithaca, NY 14850
607.277.2231

Jim Mall
907 W. Ainslie Street #1
Chicago, IL 60640
773.561.9732
malls@21stcentury.net

Mayfield Antiques of Grand Rapids
Jack Pennell
445 Bridge Street NW
Grand Rapids, MI 49504
616.451.3430

Partition Street Antiques
Richard Caggiano
114 Partition Street
Saugerties, NY 12477
845.246.1800
rcaggiano@aol.com

Peter Roberts Antiques, Inc.
Robert Melita
Peter Smorto
39 Bond Street
New York, NY 10012
212.477.9690
pra.nyc@verizon.net

Pete's Pots
Pete Maloney
5028 Rockborough Trail
Norcross, GA 30071
770.446.1419
petemaloney@mediaone.net

Preston Jordan
Jeffrey Preston
Judith A. Jordan
A. Patricia Bartinique
P.O. Box 55
Madison, NJ 07940
973.593.4860

David Rago
Suzanne Perrault
17 S. Main Street
Lambertville, NJ 08530
609.397.9374
perraggal@ragoarts.com
www.ragoarts.com

Silverman's Selected Antiques
Norman M. Silverman
6130 Boca Raton Drive
Dallas, TX 75230
214.363.6824
nsilver@aol.com

Colin C. Smith
5309 Jackson Street
Omaha, NE 68106
402.551.5018

Strictly Mission
3946 Lanark Road
Coopersburg, PA 18036
610.814.3065
www.strictlymission.com

Stuart Solomon Antiques
9 3/4 Market Street
Northampton, MA 01060
413.586.7776
antiques@ssolomon.com
www.ssolomon.com

Bruce Szopo
3860 Ellamae
Oakland, MI 48363

Phil Taylor Antiques
Phil and Kathy Taylor
224 Fox Sauk Road
Ottumwa, IA 52501
641.682.7492
ptaylorantiques@pcisa.net

John Toomey Gallery
  John Toomey
  818 North Boulevard
  Oak Park, IL 60301
  708.383.5234
  toomey@interaccess.com

Treadway Gallery
  Don Treadway
  Jerri Durham
  2029 Madison Road
  Cincinnati, OH 45208
  513.321.6742
  info@treadwaygallery.com
  www.treadwaygallery.com

20th Century Consortium
  Dan L. Lopez
  1004 Westport Road
  Kansas City, MO 64111
  816.931.0986
  Lopez4@swbell.net

Voorhees Craftsman
  Steve Voorhees
  Mary Ann Voorhees
  Three locations:
  Antique Society
    2661 Gravenstein Highway S
    Sebastopol, CA 95472
  Santa Monica Antique Market
    1607 Lincoln Boulevard
    Santa Monica, CA 90404

Large Shop
  1415 N. Lake Avenue
  Pasadena, CA 91104
  888.982.6377
  707.584.3502 fax
  vcraftsman@earthlink.net
  www.voorheescraftsman.com

PHOTO CREDITS

SELECTED BIBLIOGRAPHY

BOOKS AND CATALOG REPRINTS

A Souvenir of the Great Pan-American Exposition—May 1 to November 1, 1901. Grand Rapids, MI: James Hayne Co., 1901.

Adapting Quaint Furniture to American Needs. Grand Rapids, MI: Stickley Brothers Company, 1925.

Allwood, John. *The Great Exhibitions.* London: Macmillan Publishing Co., 1977.

Anscombe, Isabelle, and Charlotte Gere. *Arts and Crafts in Britain and America.* New York: Rizzoli International Publications, 1978.

Austin, Bruce A. *The American Arts and Crafts Movement in Western New York 1900–1920.* Rochester, NY: Rochester Institute of Technology, 1991.

Bartinique, A. Patricia. *Gustav Stickley, His Craft.* Parsippany, NJ: The Craftsman Farms Foundation, 1992.

Bavarro, Joseph J., and Thomas Mossman. *The Furniture of Gustav Stickley: History, Techniques, Projects.* New York: Van Nostrand Reinhold, 1982.

Binstead, Herbert E. *The Furniture Styles.* Chicago: Trade Periodical Co., 1909.

Boris, Eileen. Art and Labor: *Ruskin, Morris and the Craftsman Ideal in America.* Philadelphia: Temple University Press, 1986.

Bowman, Leslie Greene. *American Arts & Crafts: Virtue in Design, A Catalogue of the Palevsky/Evans Collection and Related Works in the Los Angeles County Museum of Art.* Boston: Los Angeles County Museum of Art in association with Bullfinch Press/Little, Brown and Company, 1990.

Bowman, Leslie Greene, and Anna Tobin D'Ambrosio. *The Distinction of Being Different: Joseph P. McHugh and the American Arts and Crafts Movement.* Utica, NY: Munson-Williams-Proctor Institute, 1993.

Burke, Doreen Bolger, and others. *In Pursuit of Beauty: Americans and the Aesthetic Movement.* New York: The Metropolitan Museum of Art in association with Rizzoli International Publications, 1986.

Carron, Christian G., and others. *Grand Rapids Furniture: The Story of America's Furniture City.* Grand Rapids, MI: The Public Museum of Grand Rapids, 1998.

Cathers, David M. *Furniture of the American Arts and Crafts Movement Furniture Made by Gustav Stickley, L. & J. G. Stickley and the Roycroft Shop.* Rev. ed. Philmont, NY: Turn of the Century Editions, 1996.

Cathers, David M., ed. *Gustav Stickley's Craftsman Farms: A Pictorial History.* Morris Plains, NJ: Turn of the Century Editions in association with The Craftsman Farms Press, 1999.

Cathers, David M., and Alexander Vertikoff. *Stickley Style: Arts and Crafts Homes in the Craftsman Tradition.* New York: Archetype Press, 1999.

Clark, Robert Judson, and others. *The Arts and Crafts Movement in America 1876–1916.* Princeton, NJ: Princeton University Press, 1972.

Cooper, Jeremy. *Victorian and Edwardian Décor from the Gothic Revival to Art Nouveau.* New York: Abbeville Press, 1987.

Cummings, Elizabeth, and Wendy Kaplan. *The Arts and Crafts Movement.* New York and London: Thames and Hudson, 1991.

Darling, Sharon. *Chicago Furniture: Art, Craft & Industry, 1833–1983.* New York: The Chicago Historical Society in association with W. W. Norton & Company, 1983.

Davidoff, Donald, and Stephen Gray. *Innovation and Derivation: The Contribution of L. & J. G. Stickley to the Arts and Crafts Movement.* Parsippany, NJ: The Craftsman Farms Foundation, 1995.

Davidoff, Donald A., and Robert L. Zarrow, eds. *Early L. & J. G. Stickley Furniture—From Onondaga Shops to Handcraft.* New York: Dover Publications, 1992. (Reprint of various L. & J. G. Stickley catalogs.)

Denker, Burt, ed. *The Substance of Style: Perspectives on the American Arts and Crafts Movement.* Winterthur, DE: The Henry Francis DuPont Winterthur Museum, 1996.

Descriptive Catalogue of the German Arts and Crafts at the Universal Exposition, St. Louis 1904. Imperial German Commission, 1904.

Fish, Marilyn. *Gustav Stickley 1884–1900: The Stickley Brothers, Stickley & Simonds, and the Gustav Stickley Company.* North Caldwell, NJ: Little Pond Press, 1999.

Fish, Marilyn. *Gustav Stickley: Heritage & Early Years.* North Caldwell, NJ: Little Pond Press, 1997.

Fish, Marilyn. *The New Craftsman Index.* Lambertville, NJ: Arts & Crafts Quarterly Press, 1997.

France, Jean R., and others. *A Rediscovery: Harvey Ellis Artist, Architect.* Rochester, NY: Memorial Art Gallery, 1972.

Freeman, John Crosby. *The Forgotten Rebel: Gustav Stickley and His Craftsman Mission Furniture.* Watkins Glen, NY: Turn of the Century Editions, 1990.

Gray, Stephen, and Robert Edwards, eds. *Collected Works of Gustav Stickley.* New York: Turn of the Century Editions, 1981. (Reprint of various Craftsman catalogs.)

Gray, Stephen. *The Early Work of Gustav Stickley.* New York: Turn of the Century Press, 1987. (Reprint of various Craftsman catalogs.)

Gray, Stephen, and William Porter. *Gustav Stickley After 1909.* Philmont, NY: Turn of the Century Editions, 1995. (Reprint of various Craftsman catalogs.)

Gray, Stephen, ed. *The Mission Furniture of L. & J. G. Stickley.* New York: Turn of the Century Editions, 1989. (Reprint of various L. & J. G. Stickley catalogs.)

Gray, Stephen, ed. *"Quaint" Furniture In Arts and Crafts.* New York: Turn of the Century Editions, 1988. (Reprint of Stickley Brothers catalogs.)

Greenhalgh, Paul, ed. *Art Nouveau 1890–1914.* New York: Harry N. Abrams, Inc., 2000.

Hanks, David A. *The Decorative Designs of Frank Lloyd Wright.* New York: E. P. Dutton, 1979.

Hewitt, Mark A. *Gustav Stickley's Craftsman Farms: The Quest for an Arts and Crafts Utopia.* Syracuse, NY: Syracuse University Press, 2001.

Hotel El Tovar On the Rim of the Grand Canyon. New York: Norman Pierce Company, 1909.

James, Michael L. *Drama in Design—The Life and Craft of Charles Rohlfs.* Buffalo, NY: Burchfield Art Center, 1994.

Johnson, Bruce. *The Official Price Guide to Arts and Crafts.* Second ed. New York: House of Collectibles, 1992.

Kaplan, Wendy, and others. *The Art That is Life: The Arts and Crafts Movement in America, 1875–1920.* Boston: Museum of Fine Arts, 1987.

Ludwig, Coy L. *The Arts & Crafts Movement in New York State 1890s–1920s.* Hamilton, NY: Gallery Association of New York, 1983.

Marek, Don. *Arts and Crafts Furniture Design: The Grand Rapids Contribution 1895–1915.* Ed. Peter A. Copeland and Janet H. Copeland. Grand Rapids, MI: Grand Rapids Art Museum, 1987.

Marek, Don. Introduction to *Grand Rapids Art Metalwork 1902–1918.* Grand Rapids, MI: Heartwood, 1999.

Marek, Don. *Quaint Furniture Catalog No. 42.* Ed. Peter A. Copeland and Janet H. Copeland. Parchment, MI: (Reprint of Stickley Brothers catalog.)

Marek, Don, and Richard Weidman. Introduction to *The 1912 Quaint Furniture Catalog No. 38.* Parchment, MI: Parchment Press, 1993. (Reprint of Stickley Brothers catalog.)

Mattie, Erik. *World's Fairs.* New York: Princeton Architectural Press, 1998.

Naylor, Gillian. *The Arts & Crafts Movement.* London: Studio Vista, 1971.

Quaint Furniture in Arts and Crafts. New York: Turn of the Century Editions, 1981. (Reprint of Stickley Brothers catalog.)

Ransom, Frank E. *A City Built on Wood, A History of the Furniture Industry in Grand Rapids, Michigan 1850–1950.* Ann Arbor, MI: Edwards Brothers, 1955.

Sanders, Barry. *A Complex Fate: Gustav Stickley and the Craftsman Movement.* New York: John Wiley & Sons, Inc., 1996.

Sanders, Barry, ed. *The Craftsman: An Anthology.* Salt Lake City, UT: Peregrine Smith, 1978.

Smith, Mary Ann. *Gustav Stickley: The Craftsman.* Syracuse, NY: Syracuse University Press, 1983.

Stickley Craftsman Furniture Catalogs. New York: Dover Publications, Inc., 1979. (Reprint of Craftsman and L. & J. G. Stickley Catalogs.)

Stickley, Gustav. *Craftsman Homes.* New York: Craftsman Publishing Company, 1909.

Stickley, Gustav. *More Craftsman Homes.* New York: Craftsman Publishing Company, 1912.

Stickley, Gustav. *What is Wrought in the Craftsman Workshops* (1904). New York: Turn of the Century Editions, n.d. (Reprint booklet.

The Story of a Developing Furniture Style. Fayetteville, NY: The L. & J. G. Stickley, Inc., 1950.

Volpe, Tod M., Beth Cathers and others. *Treasures of the American Arts and Crafts Movement 1890–1920.* New York: Harry N. Abrams, Inc., 1988.

The 1912 and 1915 Gustav Stickley Craftsman Furniture Catalogs. Reprint, New York: Dover Publications, Inc. in association with The Athenaeum of Philadelphia, 1991.

PERIODICALS

"Albert G. Stickley, One of the Deans Of the Furniture Industry, Has Two Displays in the Hundredth Market." *The Grand Rapids Herald,* December 26, 1927.

American Cabinet Maker and Upholsterer, 1898–1920.

"Art is Mastered: Finest 'English Morocco Furniture' Now Produced Here." *Evening Press* [Grand Rapids], June 23, 1910.

Cathers, David M. "From the Studio of LaMont A. Warner." *Style 1900,* November 1996.

Cathers, David M. "Gustav Stickley's 1900 Line." *Style 1900,* November 2001.

Cathers, David M. "Gustav Stickley, George H. Jones and the Making of Inlaid Craftsman Furniture." *Style 1900,* February 2000.

Clark, Michael, and Jill Thomas-Clark. "Gus Meets L & J. G.; Craftstyle." *Style 1900,* February 1997.

Clark, Michael, and Jill Thomas-Clark. "Gustav vs. Kaufmann Brothers." *Style 1900,* February 1997.

The Craftsman, 1901–16.

"Creditors Force Gustav Stickley Into Bankruptcy." *Syracuse Post-Standard,* March 23, 1915.

Davidoff, Donald A. "Sophisticated Design: The Mature Work of L. and J. G. Stickley." *Antiques and Fine Art,* December 1989.

The Decorative Furnisher, 1906–28.

The Decorator and Furnisher, 1882–99.

Dekorative Kunst, 1898–1907.

Deutsche Kunst und Dekoration, 1897–1906.

Edgewood, Margaret. "Some Sensible Furniture." *The House Beautiful,* October 1900.

Furniture, 1909–12.

Furniture and Decoration and The Furniture Gazette, 1892–99.

"Furniture from the Eastwood Craftsman." *The Art Interchange,* November 1901.

The Furniture Journal, 1898–1920.

The Furniture Trade Review, 1880–1919.

The Furniture World, 1900–21.

Good Furniture, 1913–28.

The Grand Rapids Furniture Record, 1900–21.

The House Beautiful, 1897–1920.

Howe, Samuel. "A Visit to the House of Mr. Stickley." *The Craftsman,* February 1903.

The International Studio, 1897–1915.

Michigan Artisan/Furniture Manufacturer and Artisan, 1880–1926.

"Quaint Furniture by Stickley Brothers Company." *The Daily News* [Grand Rapids], June 28, 1906.

Reed, Cleota. "Irene Sargent: Rediscovering A Lost Legend." *The Courier.* Syracuse Library Associates, Summer 1979.

Sargent, Irene. "A Recent Arts and Crafts Exhibition." *The Craftsman,* May 1903.

Smith, David Robertson. "Quaint Furniture." *The Grand Rapids Furniture Record,* August 1902.

Stickley, Gustav. "The Ethics of Home Furnishings." *The Craftsman,* January 1916.

Stickley, Gustav. "Furniture Based Upon Good Craftsmanship." *The Craftsman,* February 1916.

Stickley, Gustav. "The German Exhibit at the Louisiana Purchase Exposition." *The Craftsman,* August 1904.

Stickley, Gustav. "The Most Valuable of All Arts." *The Craftsman,* September 1915.

Stickley, Gustav. "The Structural Style in Cabinet-Making." *The House Beautiful,* December 1903.

Stickley, Gustav. "Thoughts Occasioned by an Anniversary: A Plea for a Democratic Art." *The Craftsman,* October 1904.

The Studio, 1893–1915.

Thomson, James. "The Intricate Elegance of Sheraton Art." *The Craftsman,* May 1915.

Upholstery Dealer and Decorative Furnisher, 1901–5.

"What of the Future." *The Grand Rapids Furniture Record,* June 1900.

ORIGINAL CATALOGS AND PAMPHLETS

Albert Stickley, Stickley Brothers Company

Quaint Furniture, 1902

Quaint Furniture by Stickley Bros. Co., 1903

Quaint Furniture. Detroit: Geo. J. Reindel & Co., n.d.

Quaint Furniture Stickley Bros. Co., n.d, about 1904–5

Quaint Specials for Sales and Advertising, n.d.

Charles Stickley, Stickley & Brandt Chair Co. and Brandt Furniture Co.

Modern Craft Styles Created and Built by Charles Stickley at the Shops of The Stickley & Brandt Chair Co., Binghamton, NY, n.d., about 1910

Stickley-Brandt Furniture Company, Catalog A, No. 5., about 1903

Stickley -Brandt Furniture Company, Satisfaction Furniture at Factory Figures, 1908.

Gustav Stickley, United Crafts, Craftsman Workshops, The Craftsman

Cabinet Work from the Craftsman Workshops, Catalogue D, n.d., about 1905.

Catalogue of Craftsman Furniture, 1909

Catalogue of Craftsman Furniture, 1910

Chips from the Craftsman Workshop. 1901 catalog.

Chips from the Craftsman Workshops. New York: Kalhoff Co., 1906.

Chips from the Craftsman Workshop. Number II, 1907.

Chips from the Workshops of the United Crafts, 1901

The Craftsman Department of Home Furnishings, n.d., about 1913.

Craftsman Furnishing, about 1905

Craftsman Furnishings for the Home, 1912

Craftsman Furniture, 1912

Craftsman Furniture, 1913

The Craftsman Workshops, Supplement to Catalog D, n.d., about 1905

The Craftsman Story, n.d., about 1905

New Furniture from the Workshop of Gustave Stickley, n.d., about 1900

Some Chips from the Craftsman Workshops, n.d. about 1909

Things Wrought by the United Crafts, about 1902

Twenty-Four Craftsman Houses, n.d., about 1910

What They Say About The Craftsman, No. 3, n.d., about 1912

Woodwork and How to Finish It, 1914

Leopold Stickley, John George Stickley, L. & J. G. Stickley

Handcraft Furniture, n.d., about 1908–10

The Work of L. & J. G. Stickley—Supplement 1912

The Work of L. & J. G. Stickley, n.d., about 1914

George Clingman, Tobey Furniture Company.

New Furniture from the Shop of The Tobey Furniture Co., Chicago, n.d., 1900.

The New Cedar Furniture: an inviting restful, artistic furniture for the home, cottage or club. Chicago: The Company, n.d.

"Russmore" Furniture. Chicago: Metcalf Stationery Co., 1902

Russmore Furniture. Chicago: The Badger Co., 1903

Some Designs in Mission Furniture For Sale by The Tobey Furniture Co., Chicago, Grand Rapids: James Bayne Co., n.d., about 1904.

CITY DIRECTORIES

Boyd's Syracuse City Directory, 1900–15.

R. L. Polk & Co.'s Grand Rapids City Directory, 1889–1930.

Trow's Business Directory of Greater New York (five Boroughs Combined), 1900–10.

Trow's General Directory of the Boroughs of Manhattan and Bronx City of New York, 1897–1916.

William's Binghamton City Directory, 1880–1929.

INDEX

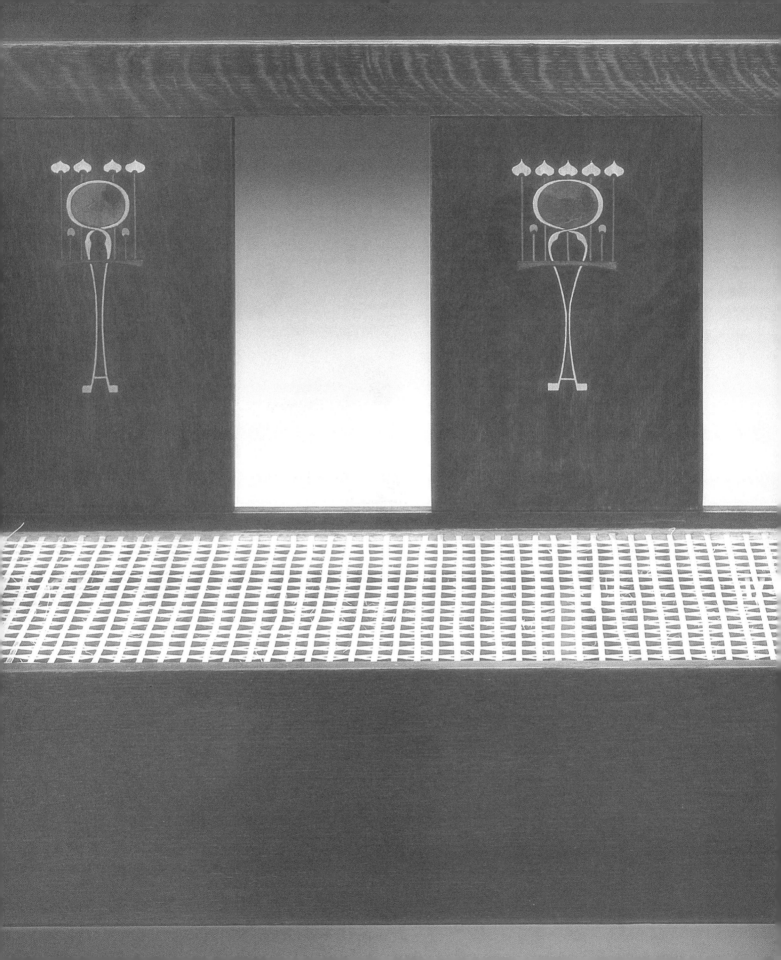